The **Asthma** Update

Alvin and Virginia Silverstein and Laura Silverstein Nunn

Titles in the DISEASE UPDATE series:

The Asthma Update
0-7660-2482-2

The Diabetes Update
0-7660-2483-0

The Flu and Pneumonia Update
0-7660-2480-6

The Sickle Cell Anemia Update
0-7660-2479-2

The STDs Update
0-7660-2484-9

The Tuberculosis Update
0-7660-2481-4

DISEASE
UPDATE

The **Asthma** Update

Alvin and Virginia Silverstein and Laura Silverstein Nunn

Enslow Publishers, Inc.
40 Industrial Road
Box 398
Berkeley Heights, NJ 07922
USA

http://www.enslow.com

Acknowledgments

The authors thank Mark F. Sands, M.D., Professor of Medicine at The University of Buffalo, and Thomas Kallstrom, Director of Respiratory Care and Biometrics at Fairview Hospital, Cleveland, for their careful reading of the manuscript and their many helpful comments and suggestions. Thanks also to Dr. Robert Strunk of the St. Louis Children's Hospital for his photograph and his many helpful suggestions.

Library of Congress Cataloging-in-Publication Data

Silverstein, Alvin.
    The asthma update / Alvin Silverstein, Virginia Silverstein, and Laura
    Silverstein Nunn.
        p. cm. — (Disease update)
    Includes bibliographical references and index.
    ISBN-10: 0-7660-2482-2 — ISBN-13: 978-0-7660-2482-2 (hardcover)
    1. Asthma—Juvenile literature. I. Silverstein, Virginia B. II. Nunn,
Laura Silverstein. III. Title. IV. Series.
RC591.S553 2006
616.2'38—dc22

                           2005018728

Printed in the United States of America

10 9 8 7 6 5 4 3 2 1

To Our Readers: We have done our best to make sure all Internet Addresses in this book were active and appropriate when we went to press. However, the author and the publisher have no control over and assume no liability for the material available on those Internet sites or on other Web sites they may link to. Any comments or suggestions can be sent by e-mail to comments@enslow.com or to the address on the back cover.

Photo Credits: © 2005 Jupiter Images Corporation, pp. 42, 43 (top, bottom), 44, 46 (middle, bottom), 47, 53, 63, 80, 81 (middle, bottom), 84, 85, 86, 97; AJPhoto / Photo Researchers, Inc., p. 70; Alex Bartel / Photo Researchers, p. 46 (top); American Academy of Allergy, Asthma and Immunology, pp. 38, 57; AP/WideWorld, pp. 8, 13, 17, 20, 22, 28, 31, 45, 58, 65, 95, 99; Courtesy of the Alan Mason Chesney Medical Archives of John Hopkins Medical, pp. 25, 109; Courtesy of the National Library of Medicine, p. 108; © Dr. Dennis Kunkel / Visuals Unlimited, p. 43 (middle); Enslow Publishers, Inc., p. 50; Grapes - Michaud / Photo Researchers, Inc., p. 36; © Larry Stepanowicz / Visuals Unlimited, p. 81 (top); Lea Paterson / Science Photo Library, p. 91; Life Art image copyright 1998 Lippincott Williams & Wilkins. All rights reserved., pp. 34, 51, 110; Mark Clarke / Photo Researchers, Inc., p. 72; © Ralph Hutchings/Visuals Unlimited, pp. 5, 7; Strominger Professor of Pediatrics, Washington University School of Medicine, Division of Allergy and Pulmonary Medicine, St. Louis Children's Hospital, p. 78; Tracy C. McFadden, p. 82.

Cover Photo: © Ralph Hutchings/Visuals Unlimited

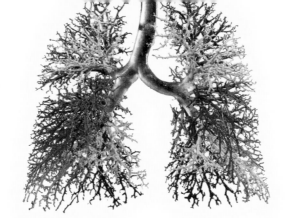

Contents

Asthma

What is it?
A lung condition in which the airways become inflamed (swollen). This causes the air passages to become narrow, which makes breathing difficult.

Who gets it?
Both sexes; all ages; all races. In children, boys are more likely than girls to develop asthma. In adults, asthma is slightly more common in women than men. Asthma is also more common in African Americans and Hispanics than Caucasians.

How do you get it?
No one knows for sure. People may inherit a tendency to develop asthma. Asthma attacks (episodes) may be triggered by air pollution (including cigarette smoke), plant pollens, animal dander, dust mites, cockroach droppings, and molds, as well as cold air and exercise. Infections, including the common cold, may also trigger or worsen asthma attacks.

What are the symptoms?
Coughing, wheezing, a feeling of tightness in the chest, and shortness of breath during episodes. Attacks often occur during the night.

How is it treated?

Handheld inhalers containing anti-inflammatory drugs can keep asthma under control; drugs that widen the air passages are used to stop episodes or prevent exercise-induced asthma. Allergy shots can make asthma patients less sensitive to allergy triggers. Avoiding known triggers is also important in managing asthma.

How can it be prevented?

Avoiding asthma triggers can prevent most episodes; air conditioners and air filters can reduce the effects of air pollution. Taking medication exactly according to the treatment plan and working closely with a health-care provider can help prevent episodes.

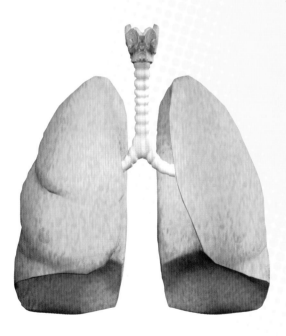

Country music singer Wynonna Judd performs for her fans during a concert in 1999. She was first diagnosed with asthma when she was eight years old.

1

Out of Breath

Country singer Wynonna Judd started her career at the age of eighteen. She went from being a typical teenager to riding around on a tour bus with her mother, Naomi Judd, the other half of the country duo The Judds. Just a few years later, The Judds were a huge sensation. They were selling out concerts and their album had gone platinum. Being in the public eye all the time would be a challenge for anyone. But Wynonna also had to deal with her own private challenge—asthma.

Wynonna was first diagnosed with asthma when she was eight years old. She vividly remembers the asthma attacks she would get as a young child: "It would usually start with a coughing fit, then I'd get sweaty and hot under the collar, then my chest would tighten until it felt like there was a cinder block on it. I'd fight for air, like a drowning person underwater. Eventually the attack would subside. But there was always another one."[1]

Wynonna's asthma was triggered by a variety of things—cigarette smoke, humidity, exercise, and sometimes animal fur. There were times when she had no idea what set it off. No one in Wynonna's immediate family had asthma. But she did have a cousin, Cynthia, who died from a severe asthma attack when she was only twelve years old. Sometimes Wynonna's asthma would get so severe that she'd have to go to the hospital. When Wynonna was young, her family was rather poor and could not afford the best treatment for her condition. Wynonna used an inhaler and prescription pills when she had an attack. During her teens, she started using her inhaler as many as six times a day. (When a person uses an inhaler that often, it usually means that the asthma is not being managed properly.)

When Wynonna became a country superstar, she tried to hide her asthma. Thousands of fans depended on her. She couldn't let them down. Sometimes she'd even have an attack during her concerts. One time as she stood in front of a sold-out crowd of 70,000 people, Wynonna waited for the lights to dim, turned around briefly, and quickly took a puff from her inhaler. Then she continued singing. She thought she was handling her asthma fine on her own. It seemed normal to her to end up in the hospital twice a year from asthma attacks.

For many years, Wynonna remained in denial about the seriousness of her disease. It was not until after her son Elijah was born (in 1994) that Wynonna started to treat her asthma properly. She started to exercise and eat healthier foods. She lost some weight, and her asthma seemed to get better. The following year, however, she gained the weight back when she became pregnant with her daughter Grace (born in 1995).

> Worldwide, as many as 300 million people have asthma.

Her asthma started to get worse again. Finally, Wynonna went to a doctor, who gave her a prescription for a preventative asthma medicine. She takes the medicine every day to stop the attacks before they start. She also committed herself to a healthy diet and exercise program.

Thanks to proper treatment, Wynonna has been free of asthma attacks since 1998 (at age thirty-four).

However, around the same time, Elijah was also diagnosed with asthma. Wynonna knew something was not right when Elijah started to have terrible coughing fits. His condition got so bad that he had to go to the hospital a number of times. Wynonna was heartbroken watching her son go through what she did as a child. She took him to a doctor so that he, too, could start taking preventative medicine. Now he and his mother can both breathe a little easier.[2]

Asthma is a lung condition that causes swelling in a person's airways (breathing passages). As the airways become narrow, it becomes difficult to push air out of the lungs. As a result, the person may have trouble breathing and may cough or wheeze. (Wheezing is a whistling sound a person makes when he or she breathes.) This series of events—swelling in the airways, breathing difficulty, and coughing or wheezing—is called an asthma attack. It may also be called an asthma flare-up, or episode. Asthma attacks are usually brought on by "triggers"—things that set off an attack. Dust, mold, or pollen in the air may bring on breathing problems.

> Asthma can occur at any age, but most often it first appears in childhood.

Famous People with Asthma

Name	Occupation
Avril Lavigne	Singer, songwriter
Billy Joel	Singer
Bob Hope	Actor, comedian
Charles Dickens	Author
Coolio	Rap singer
Dennis Rodman	NBA basketball player
Elizabeth Taylor	Actress
Emmitt Smith	Pro football player
Greg Louganis	Olympic gold medalist (diving)
Jackie Joyner-Kersee	Olympic gold medalist (track and field)
Jason Alexander	Actor
Jerome Bettis	Pro football player
John F. Kennedy	35th president of the United States
Liza Minnelli	Actress, singer
Ludwig van Beethoven	Classical composer
Martin Scorsese	Film director
Nancy Hogshead	Olympic gold medalist (swimming)
Patrick Kennedy	Congressman from Rhode Island
Sharon Stone	Actress
Theodore Roosevelt	26th president of the United States

Avril Lavigne

Coolio

Air pollution, very cold weather, exercise, or even a bad cold can also be triggers.

Asthma is a common problem. Worldwide, as many as 300 million people have asthma.[3] Over the years, asthma cases have been increasing steadily. According to the *Global Burden of Asthma* report released in February 2004, the number of people with asthma worldwide may rise to 400 million in twenty years.[4] In the United States alone, asthma affects 20 million people.[5] About 5 million of them are children.[6]

Asthma can occur at any age, but most often it first appears in childhood. More and more children are developing asthma than ever before. Many people think that kids grow out of asthma, but usually children with asthma have to live with it for the rest of their lives.

Without proper treatment, asthma attacks can be very dangerous—even deadly. About 5,400 Americans die every year from asthma.[7] There is no cure, but there are ways to keep the condition under control. Symptoms can be treated with fast-acting medications. There are medicines that, when taken daily, can prevent attacks. Avoiding triggers is also an important part of managing asthma. People with asthma can live long, productive lives.

2

Asthma in History

Theodore Roosevelt was a remarkable man. He was a soldier, a hunter, a conservationist, and president of the United States. He was a strong leader and earned the respect of the American people, who affectionately called him Teddy. Toy makers created teddy bears in honor of the president, after word got out that Roosevelt refused to shoot a bear cub during a hunting trip.

Roosevelt lived an adventurous life. He was full of energy and loved the outdoors. He enjoyed horseback riding, swimming, hunting, hiking, and boxing. It is hard to believe that this strong, active man had been a weak, sickly boy through much of his childhood.

Growing up, "Teedie," as his family called him, was in and out of hospitals because of his severe asthma episodes. He was often bedridden with a chronic cough. He could not even go to school regularly. He had to be schooled at home, where he learned to love reading and writing.

During Roosevelt's time (in the 1800s), asthma was not fully understood. There were no inhalers or special medicines to treat the disease. Doctors offered the only treatments they knew—anything from vacations on the coast to drinking coffee. (The chemicals in coffee were believed to open up breathing passages.) Teedie's parents tried everything the doctors suggested, but nothing worked. Teedie's father spent many hours in his son's bedroom talking and reading to him, trying to help him through his asthma attacks.

At twelve years of age, Teedie's father told him that he needed a strong body as well as a strong mind to develop fully. His father built a small gym in their house to build up Teedie's strength. Young Roosevelt was determined. He worked hard and exercised regularly. He also took boxing lessons. Eventually, Teedie's asthma improved. He had fewer attacks, and they were much less severe than before. Although he could not eliminate

Doctors were unable to help young Theodore Roosevelt's asthma. But with regular exercise, he had fewer and less severe asthma attacks. He is shown here at age seventeen.

his asthma, Roosevelt made it so manageable that he was able to live an active, productive life.[1]

An Age-Old Illness

Although asthma was a mystery during Theodore Roosevelt's time, it was not a new disease. In fact, it has been around for thousands of years.

An asthma-like condition was described as early as 1550 B.C. in an Egyptian document called the Ebers Papyrus. This ancient document contains medical descriptions and treatments of various illnesses and conditions. It includes a remedy for asthma that involved a mixture of herbs heated on a brick so that the patient could breathe in its fumes. This was supposed to help open the breathing passages. Some other suggested treatments were much less appealing, such as swallowing camel and crocodile droppings!

The Chinese described asthma in a medical textbook dating from 1000 B.C. The ancient Chinese used an herb, ma huang, to treat asthma. Ma huang contains ephedrine, a chemical that opens up the airways. It was not until 1924 that ephedrine was finally brought to the West, where it was used as an asthma treatment. It remained a standard treatment for decades until it was replaced with newer drugs. Drugs similar to ephedrine are still used in medications to relieve nasal congestion.

Around 400 B.C., Greek physician Hippocrates named the condition *asthma*, from the Greek word meaning "panting." He used this term to describe the wheezing sound that asthma patients make, which is the most recognizable symptom of the disease. Hippocrates believed that asthma was caused by an

> Asthma is not a new disease. In fact, it has been
> ....
> around for thousands of years.

imbalance of bodily fluids. His recommended treatment included induced vomiting, purging, and bleeding.

In A.D. 200, another Greek physician, Galen, documented the clinical signs of asthma. He observed that breathing problems occurred after strenuous exercise or any other type of work. It caused flushed cheeks and bulging eyes, as if the person were being strangled. Galen also noticed an overproduction of mucus in

Struggling for Air

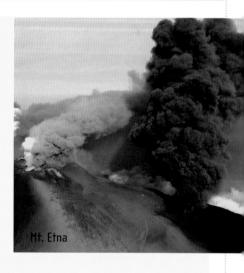

Mt. Etna

Imagine a group of eight to ten people, around the end of the second century A.D., dressed in robes and sandals. They have just sailed the treacherous seas from their homeland in Greece to the island of Sicily. Once they arrived, they proceeded to hike up the 10,900-foot- (3,320-meter)-high Mt. Etna. This feat would have been difficult enough for anyone, but imagine that these hikers have asthma. Those who manage to make it to top, wheezing all the way, are greeted by an active volcano blowing out sulfurous smoke that irritates the hikers' already hypersensitive airways. Their lungs are filling up with mucus, making them gasp desperately for air. That sounds pretty horrifying, but it was actually a treatment for asthma prescribed by the Greek physician Galen. The sulfurous fumes were supposed to loosen the mucus in the airways so that it could be coughed up and spit out. (The ancient accounts that describe this treatment do not give statistics on how many of Galen's patients managed to get off the mountain alive.)[2]

people with asthma. He explained that when breathing sounded harsh, it could be an indication of a buildup of fluids (mucus), which get stuck in the airways and cannot be easily loosened. One of his suggested treatments was drinking owl's blood in wine.

One of the earliest attempts to treat asthma with medicine was made in the A.D. 600s, by Paul of Aegina, a Greek physician who practiced in Alexandria, Egypt. He gave patients specific medicines to break up the mucus plugs so that the mucus could easily be coughed up.

In 1160, Maimonides, a famous Jewish physician and philosopher, observed that the condition seemed to run in families. This suggested that heredity may be responsible for the occurrence of asthma. He also talked about various triggers of asthma attacks. His remedies included living in a dry climate and eating lots of chicken soup.

A sixteenth-century physician named Jerome Cardan treated King Edward VI of England after the king suffered an asthma episode. The king seemed to be cured once the doctor removed the feather pillows from his bed. This was the first documented connection between asthma and allergies.

In 1698, an English physician, Sir John Floyer, published, *A Treatise of the Asthma*, in which he wrote about his own asthma symptoms, as well those of his

Where There's Smoke . . .

Sir Walter Raleigh brought tobacco to England from the Americas in 1585. Amazingly, smoking tobacco was soon recommended for treating asthma and other respiratory problems. This misguided idea was still around in the mid-1800s, when doctors recommended smoking cigars as a "cure" for Theodore Roosevelt's asthma. Today's doctors know that tobacco smoke can actually make asthma worse.

patients. He came to the conclusion that asthma was caused by muscle contractions in the bronchi (airways). This was the first medical description of the underlying cause of asthma.

In 1860, Henry Hyde Salter, a London physician, recommended drinking strong black coffee to treat asthma. The caffeine in coffee is related chemically to theophylline, which is now used in asthma medicines. Theophylline was isolated from cocoa in 1888. Before inhalers were developed, people with asthma had to chew bitter-tasting theophylline tablets.

In 1903, adrenaline (epinephrine) was used in asthma treatment. The drug was injected into the skin. It was not until 1929 that epinephrine was first administered by an inhaler at Guy's Hospital in London.

Even though more effective asthma treatments were starting to become available, the cause of asthma still remained a mystery. If medical experts could solve this mystery, they would be able to develop drugs that could attack the underlying cause, in addition to treating the narrowing airways.

Searching for a Cause

For years, people offered a variety of theories to explain the cause of asthma. One popular idea was that asthma was caused by stress. In 1939, a Denver-based medical center called the National Home for Jewish Children offered a program for children whose asthma seemed hopeless and unmanageable. The head of the program, Dr. M. Murray Peshkin, an allergy specialist, noticed that in many cases, children with severe asthma seemed to improve immediately after being taken away from their home environment. He thought that perhaps the parents were to blame. He viewed the disease as an emotional reaction to stress in the family. Dr. Peshkin believed that a separation of as long as two years was needed for a lasting cure.

In 1951, the Home hired its first full-time medical director, Dr. Allan Hurst. Hurst questioned Dr. Peshkin's theories and set out to prove that asthma was not just an "emotional" illness. He found that important changes in the body happen during an asthma episode. These changes affect the immune system, which normally defends the body against disease germs. Dr. Hurst reported his research findings to the American Medical Association in 1951.

In 1957, the Home set up a new asthma research facility called the Children's Asthma Research Institute and Hospital (CARIH). Researchers continued to try to disprove Dr. Peshkin's theory.

In 1966, a husband-and-wife team at CARIH, Kimishige and Teruko Ishizaka, made a major research breakthrough. They discovered immunoglobulin E (IgE), known as the "allergy antibody." They found that many people who had asthma had larger amounts of IgE in their blood than people without asthma. People with asthma were more sensitive to their environment than nonallergic people.

Kimishige and Teruko Ishizaka found large amounts of IgE in the blood of people with asthma. This allergy antibody makes people with asthma more sensitive to their environments.

Also in the 1960s, Dr. Irving Itkin reported that the basic problem in asthma is the hypersensitive airways in the lungs, sometimes called "twitchy lungs." This was additional evidence that asthma was not the result of emotional stress. It was then observed, however, that although stress does not cause asthma, it can trigger asthma symptoms—but only in someone who already has twitchy lungs.

By the 1970s, researchers had discovered common triggers of asthma, such as allergens (plant pollens, animal dander, dusts, molds, etc.), histamine, cold air, cigarette smoke, air pollution, exercise, and emotional reactions. Researchers also showed that not all asthma patients are allergic, and not all allergic people have asthma. Allergy is just one of many triggers of asthma.

By the late 1980s, asthma specialists had become aware that airway inflammation plays a key role in the disease. Lack of awareness of this factor and poor treatment were actually contributing to asthma deaths.

In 1991, the National Institutes of Health issued new guidelines for the diagnosis and treatment of asthma. They stressed the importance of treating inflammation as the new focus.

3

What Is Asthma?

Anyone who tries to tackle Jerome Bettis during a football game quickly feels as if they have been hit by a bus. That is why fans and teammates call him "the Bus." As running back for the Pittsburgh Steelers, Bettis plows through oncoming players. The only thing that might be able to slow down "the Bus" is asthma.

Jerome Bettis was diagnosed with asthma in 1986, when he was fourteen years old. He had just made the high school football team. "I was working out on a track, getting ready to go through practice, and I actually got a little dizzy," Bettis recalls. "My coach was a little nervous so he had them take me to the doctor, and my

Jerome Bettis, Pittsburgh Steelers running back, sprints for a touchdown. Bettis must monitor his asthma closely to avoid an attack on the field.

family met me there. . . . That's when it all started." The first thought he had after hearing the diagnosis was about football. "I can't play anymore," he thought. "That's the end of it." But his parents did not want him to give up his dreams. "Hey, you can do whatever you want to do as long as you just manage it," his parents told him.[1] His family knew about asthma because his older brother had it as well.

Throughout high school, Bettis did a good job keeping his asthma under control. He took medication every day and used an inhaler when he needed to. And he continued to play football. In fact, the local newspaper, the *Detroit Free Press*, named him as one of the top high school players in Michigan. Bettis continued his football career in college, making a name for himself on the Notre Dame football team. In 1993, he was drafted by the Los Angeles Rams, which later moved to St. Louis. In 1996, he started playing for the Pittsburgh Steelers. His asthma still seemed to be under control. But Bettis admits that after high school, he did not pay as close attention to his asthma as he should have.[2] He had to learn the hard way that asthma does not go away, even when you are symptom-free. In 1997, Bettis had an asthma attack during a televised game between the Pittsburgh Steelers and the Jacksonville Jaguars. Struggling for air, Bettis somehow made it to the sideline. There he told the doctors what was happening. They immediately gave him a shot to open his airways. He also had a nebulizer (breathing) treatment.

This was a wake-up call for Bettis. His fight against asthma was not over. He would have to deal with this disease for the rest of his life. Now Bettis pays close attention to his asthma. He avoids triggers, such as smoke, and he takes preventative medicine twice every day. He also keeps an inhaler with him at all times. He takes a break when he needs to, as well, even if it is during practice or during a game.

In 1999, Bettis joined a national campaign called Asthma All-Stars to educate the public about asthma, especially kids. Other members include Olympic runner Jackie Joyner-Kersee and Olympic swimmer Amy Van Dyken. In an interview, Bettis explains, "I just tell kids, it's not the end of the world to be asthmatic. You can still grow up to do the things you want to do. You can swim, run, play football, baseball, basketball, be a cheerleader, all because you're monitoring and managing your asthma."[3]

Olympic Gold Medalist Jackie Joyner-Kersee is a member of the Asthma All-Stars. If asthma is managed carefully, you can still succeed in sports.

Twitchy Lungs

Asthma, also known as bronchial asthma, is a condition that causes inflammation in the bronchial tubes (airways) in the lungs. As the airways become inflamed (red and swollen), the space inside them becomes narrow, reducing the amount of air that flows through them. This can make breathing very difficult.

Asthma is a condition that causes the lung airways to become narrow. This can make breathing very difficult.

People with asthma have airways that are overly sensitive, "twitchy," or hyperreactive. Their airways tend to overreact when foreign substances, such as dust or smoke, are breathed in. This overreaction stimulates an immune response. The body's defenders, the immune system, are called into action to defend against the foreign invaders, which results in inflammation and breathing difficulty.

Asthma is a chronic disease. That means that it is usually a lifelong problem. However, its effects are reversible. If asthma is treated and managed properly, the symptoms can be reduced or even eliminated. But the disease cannot be cured. Although the symptoms may disappear for a while, they can come back at any time. That is what happened to Jerome Bettis. As Bettis found out, asthma is still there, even when the symptoms are not.

How Does Normal Breathing Work?

Take a deep breath and let it out. Usually you do not have to think about taking a breath. In fact, you may not even realize you are doing it. Breathing becomes noticeable when you are running to catch a bus or sick with a cold. People with asthma *do* have to think about breathing, every single day. They know what it is like to struggle just to take a breath. Before you can understand what asthma is all about, first you need to understand how normal breathing works.

When you breathe in, or inhale, air comes in through your nose and mouth. The air then passes down into the lungs. The lungs are two spongy organs in your chest that fill up with air, like balloons. Inside the lungs, oxygen—an invisible gas that is part of the air—passes into your blood, which carries it to the

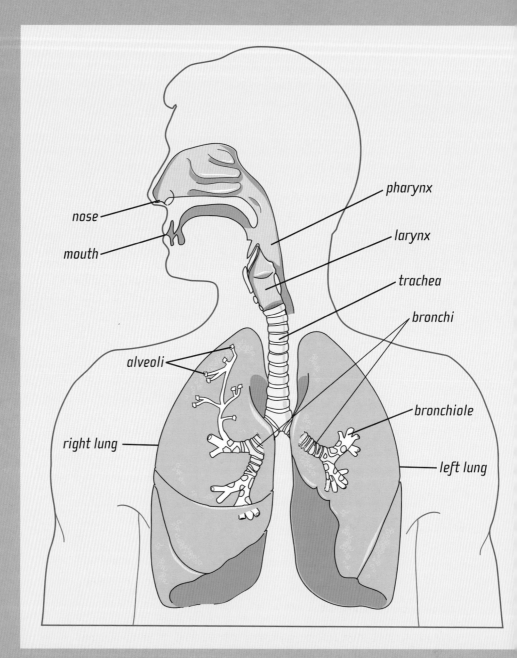

Air passes from the mouth or nose to the trachea, bronchi, and into the lungs. The air then travels into the smaller bronchioles and the tiny alveoli, where oxygen and carbon dioxide are exchanged between blood and air.

many cells of your body. Your body needs oxygen to produce energy you need for running, playing, eating, thinking, and even sleeping. When the cells use oxygen to produce energy, they also make a gas called carbon dioxide. The blood carries carbon dioxide to the lungs, and it is pushed out when you breathe out, or exhale. When you breathe in again, the process is repeated, and fresh air again enters the lungs.

The parts of the body involved in breathing make up the respiratory system. The respiratory system looks like an upside-down tree. The air you breathe goes down your throat (the pharynx) and continues down the main breathing tube, or trachea. You can feel the trachea at the front of your throat. The trachea branches to form two large tubes, called bronchi, which lead into the right and left lungs. The bronchi branch into smaller, almost threadlike tubes, called bronchioles, which look like twigs on a tree.

The bronchi and bronchioles are wrapped in bands of muscle. When these muscles relax, the airways widen. When they contract, or tighten, the airways narrow and less air can flow through. Normally when you breathe, these muscles are loose and relaxed.

The bronchioles lead into millions of tiny balloonlike air sacs in the lungs called alveoli. They look like tiny bunches of grapes, but they are too small to see without a microscope. This is where the exchange of oxygen and carbon dioxide takes place.

The airways have built-in defenses to protect the lungs from foreign particles that may be breathed in with the air. Some particles that enter your nose get trapped in bristly hairs inside your nostrils. Anything that gets past this first line of defense falls into the mucus that covers the lining of your nose. Mucus is also produced in the airways, and it picks up pollen grains or

Blowing Like the Wind

When your lungs are working properly, you can blow air out of them with as much force as the winds in a hurricane. When you sneeze, for example, air explodes out of your airways at a speed of 100 miles (160 kilometers) per hour. The air from a cough travels even faster—as much as 500 miles (805 km) per hour!

tiny bits of dust that might have gotten through. Some of the cells lining the airways have tiny hairlike structures called cilia. Cilia move back and forth continuously, creating waves in the mucus coating. Like a conveyor belt, the moving mucus sweeps trapped particles up and away from your lungs. The particles leave your body when you blow your nose, sneeze, or cough.

What Happens During an Asthma Attack?

An asthma attack, or episode, is a sudden worsening of the symptoms. A person with asthma can have symptoms, such as coughing or wheezing, from time to time. These symptoms may be mild and may not interfere with normal activities. But sometimes, the symptoms may suddenly get worse, building up to a full-blown asthma attack.

What does an asthma attack feel like? If you've never had one, try running in place for two minutes. When the time is up, pinch your nose and put a straw in your mouth. Then try to breathe in and out only through the straw. You will find that breathing, which seemed so natural before, suddenly becomes more difficult. Now narrow the straw by pinching it in the middle. Breathing becomes even *more* difficult. This is what people with

Why asthma makes it hard to breathe

Air enters the respiratory system from the nose and mouth and travels through the bronchial tubes.

In a non-asthmatic person, the muscles around the bronchial tubes are relaxed and the tissue thin, allowing for easy airflow.

In an asthmatic person, the muscles of the bronchial tubes tighten and thicken, and the air passages become inflamed and mucus-filled, making it difficult for air to move.

Inflamed bronchial tube of an asthmatic

Normal bronchial tube

Source: American Academy of Allergy, Asthma and Immunology

asthma feel when they try to breathe during an asthma attack.

So what actually happens during an asthma attack? When the bronchial tubes of a person with asthma are exposed to things like smoke or dust, they may become irritated. In an effort to prevent the particles from getting farther into the lungs, the muscles that wrap around the airways tighten. The contracting muscles make the airways narrower, leaving less room for air to get through. This effect is called a bronchospasm.

At the same time, the walls of the bronchial tubes become inflamed and swollen, making it even harder for air to flow through them. The inflammation causes the airways to produce a lot of extra mucus. Sometimes the mucus forms plugs in the airways, which blocks them even more.

What Are the Symptoms?

When the airways are narrowed, breathing becomes difficult, and a person may have *shortness of breath* or *rapid breathing. Wheezing* is the most obvious symptom of asthma. When air tries to squeeze through the narrow passageway, it makes a whistling sound, something like an out-of-tune harmonica. Wheezing tends to get worse at night. Not all people with asthma wheeze, though, which may make it hard to identify the condition. (In a severe attack, so little air may be flowing that the wheezing is too quiet to hear.) Some people feel *tightness in their chest* because their lungs have to work harder than usual to push air through the narrow airways.

Coughing is the most common symptom of asthma. It may be caused by the extra mucus and the irritation in the airways. Bronchospasms alone can also cause coughing. Unfortunately, people usually do not see coughing as a sign of something as serious as asthma. They may think it is caused by a cold or by something in their throat.

Asthma symptoms vary greatly from person to person. Each asthma episode can be different even for the same person. The symptoms can be mild, moderate, or severe. It all depends on how seriously the airways are blocked. If the asthma episode is treated quickly, further inflammation of the airways can be prevented. Then the episode may be mild. Sometimes, however, inflammation and spasm are so severe that it is too late for first-aid treatment. Then it is time to go to the emergency room. Although it is rare, a severe asthma episode can lead to death.

It is important to treat asthma attacks early. If asthma is not treated right away, the attacks may destroy some of the cilia that sweep particles away from the lungs. Then, with fewer cilia, the airway lining cannot clear out the particles as effectively. The longer the asthma

> Coughing is the most common symptom of asthma. Unfortunately, people usually do not see coughing as a sign of something as serious as asthma. They may think it is caused by a cold or by something in their throat.

is out of control, the greater the chances of a severe attack, and the longer it may take for the lungs to heal.

What Triggers an Asthma Attack?

Asthma triggers are things that start the symptoms of an asthma attack. Triggers may be substances that are inhaled, touched, eaten, or injected. Asthma attacks can even be triggered by physical or emotional factors, such as laughing or crying. No matter what the trigger, the result is the same. An asthma attack usually occurs in a person either right away or within about fifteen to thirty minutes after that person is exposed to a trigger. Sometimes, an attack can occur hours later.

Asthma is often linked with allergies. In fact, about 70 percent of asthma cases are triggered by allergies.[4] However, people with allergies do not necessarily develop asthma.

While most asthma episodes are triggered by allergies, there are also many different nonallergenic things that can set them off. Common asthma triggers (allergenic and nonallergenic) include the following:

 **House dust.** Dust can be found anywhere—on beds, carpets, bookshelves, curtains, even stuffed toys. House dust is made up of lots of things that could make you sneeze—flakes of dead skin, pollen grains, pet hair, mold spores, and little bits of insects. But an allergy to dust is probably caused by dust mites. Dust mites are microscopic creatures that live in carpets, pillows, mattresses, and bedding. They feed on dead skin flakes and other things in dust. It is usually the dust mites' droppings that cause allergy problems.

They are so tiny and light that they can easily float through the air, enter the nose, and cause symptoms.

Pollens. Hay fever is a very common allergy. It is usually caused by pollen from plants, especially from grass, trees, and ragweed. Pollen contains tiny powdery particles that plants use to make seeds.  One ragweed plant can make 8 billion pollen grains. These pollen grains are very light and can be easily carried through the air by the wind.

 **Molds.** Some people are allergic to molds. Molds are a kind of fungus that feed on rotting plant or animal matter. They can grow almost anywhere, especially in dark, moist places. You have probably seen mold growing on old bread or on old leftovers in the refrigerator. Mold makes huge numbers of spores, which are kind of like seeds. Spores are very tiny and light, just like pollen. And like pollen grains, spores are carried on the air we breathe.

Animal dander and droppings. A person who develops asthma symptoms after petting a dog or cat may be allergic to animal dander, tiny flakes of skin.

Animals shed dander on carpets and furniture. Different animals have different dander, so a person may be allergic to cats but not to dogs, or vice versa. Cats continually wash themselves, sending allergens—allergy-causing materials—into the air. Both their saliva and their dander contain allergens. Some people are allergic to bird feathers and droppings. Mice, hamsters, and guinea pigs can cause problems as well. Their urine contains a substance that may cause an allergic reaction. Another animal that can cause allergy problems is not a pet, but a pest—cockroaches. Many people are allergic to the substances in cockroach droppings. In cities, wild mice, rats, and cockroaches are a big cause of asthma.

Foods. Foods can sometimes bring on an asthma attack. Common food allergies include milk products, fish, peanuts and other nuts, wheat, and eggs. These episodes are usually part of more general  reactions that can include hives, vomiting, and diarrhea.

Irritating substances. Some irritating substances are not allergy-related. They could bring on an asthma attack in anyone with hypersensitive airways. These include tobacco smoke, chimney smoke, air pollution, automobile fumes, and certain chemicals. The amounts of irritating pollutants in the air vary, depending on the place, the time of day, and weather conditions. When general air pollution is very high, it may form a gray-brown smog that makes breathing

How Clean Is Your Air?

Air pollution is usually the worst in cities, where large numbers of cars, trucks, and factories send irritating gases and particulates into the air. One of the most polluted places in the world is Mexico City, which is surrounded by mountains that trap pollution and prevent it from being blown away. The amount of ozone in the air that people in Mexico City breathe is rated as "unhealthy" by World Health Organization standards more than three hundred days each year![5] The worst air pollution in the United States is found in the Los Angeles area. Other California cities, as well as Pittsburgh (Pennsylvania), Cleveland (Ohio), Chicago (Illinois), Detroit (Michigan), and Houston and Dallas (Texas) also rank high.[6] You can see how your home neighborhood rates by checking Environmental Defense's Scorecard on the Internet at: <http://www.scorecard.org>.

very difficult. The U.S. Environmental Protection Agency (EPA) and state environmental agencies continuously measure the amounts of five important pollutants in the air: carbon monoxide, nitrogen dioxide, ozone, particulates (solid particles of dust and soot), and sulfur dioxide. Their concentrations are compared to the national health standards to calculate an overall Air Quality Index (AQI). The AQI ratings are expressed

in words like "good," "unhealthy," and "hazardous."

Infections. An upper respiratory infection, such as a cold or flu, can trigger an asthma attack.

Weather. Weather can affect people with asthma in different ways. An asthma attack may occur when the weather is really cold or really dry. Weather extremes, from

hot to cold or vice versa, can bring on an episode as well. Walking out of your warm, cozy home into cold, wintry

weather can make your bronchial tubes contract, making breathing difficult.

Strong emotion. Stress can bring on an asthma attack. Worrying about the symptoms can even make them worse. Other emotional reactions, such as crying or laughing, can set off an attack. Emotions do not cause asthma; they can trigger attacks only in people who already have the disease.

Exercise. Exercise is a common asthma trigger. In fact, it is so common that health experts have named the

Too Clean for Our Own Good?

Some health experts say that more and more people are developing allergies and asthma because the environment is much cleaner today than it was years ago. In the past, kids grew up playing outdoors and slept with the windows open. Now, houses are air-conditioned and better insulated, kids spend more time indoors, and people rely heavily on antibacterial cleansers. Actually, it is exposure to germs that helps children build up immunity to diseases. When children are exposed to a lot of germs early in life, their body defenses get stronger. Their immune systems also learn to react more to harmful things and less to harmless things. When children grow up in an environment that is too clean, their immune systems may not get enough learning experience and overreact to harmless things like pollen or dust.

condition "exercise-induced bronchospasm," or EIB. Over 80 percent of kids with asthma have EIB.[7] Usually getting exercise is considered to be healthy, but in people with EIB, it can be dangerous.

> It is important to treat asthma attacks early. The longer the asthma is out of control, the greater the chances of a severe attack, and the longer it may take for the lungs to heal.

When people exercise, their muscles use up extra oxygen. Then their lungs have to work harder, breathing faster and taking in more air. During exercise, the nose does not have enough time to warm up the air before it goes to the lungs. The air may be cold and dry when it gets to the lungs. The cold air entering the airways may make them suddenly get narrow. As dry air passes through them, the airways lose the moist mucus that normally protects them. Since people with asthma have very sensitive airways, cold, dry air is likely to bring on an attack.

4

What Causes Asthma?

Not many people have heard of Tristan da Cunha. It is a tiny, remote island in the middle of the South Atlantic Ocean, between Africa and South America. Of all the inhabited islands in the world, Tristan da Cunha is the most remote. It is 1,200 miles (1,930 km) from the closest human-inhabited island, and 2,000 miles (3,220 km) from the mainland (South Africa). Tristan da Cunha may not be well known to the general public, but it has made a name for itself in the medical community. It holds proof of a link between asthma and heredity.

In the 1940s, a physician in the British navy visited Tristan da Cunha. The British physician was surprised

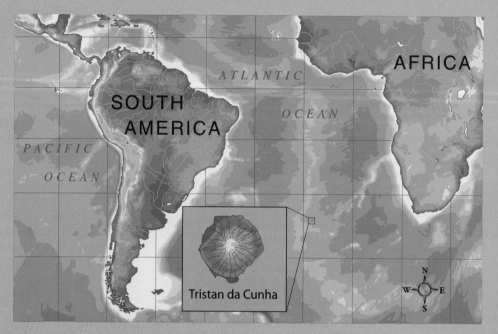

On the remote island Tristan da Cunha, 44 percent of the inhabitants have asthma. Because all of the inhabitants are now related to one another, many of the people are genetically prone to develop asthma.

to learn that 97 of its 222 inhabitants had asthma—an amazing 44 percent of the population. What made these people so susceptible? The answer was in their genes. The islanders were biologically one big family. The first settlers came to Tristan da Cunha in 1816. They included just four people—William Glass, his wife Susanna, and two other men. Over the next 130 years, only eight new women and five new men came to the island. So at the time of the medical study, all 222 people living on the island were descended from just eight men and nine women. Inbreeding between cousins could not be avoided, and therefore, by 1946, all the people were related to one another.

The British physician wrote down his observations: "There is no doubt as to the hereditary nature of the [asthma] condition. Whole families are involved and the asthmatic trait can be traced in the pedigrees through the generations. The evidence seems to point to Glass [and his wife] as the originators of the condition. The islanders themselves are of the opinion that these two persons were the original sufferers."[1]

What Are Genes?

The color of your hair, the shape of your ears, how tall you will grow—nearly all of your features—are inherited from your parents. The "instruction book" for forming all these features is contained in chemicals called DNA, found inside each of your body cells. Your DNA contains many tiny units called genes. Some of your genes came from your mother, and some from your father. That is why some of your features are like your mother's and some are like your father's—and some may be a combination of both.

DNA

All in the Family

Scientists are not sure exactly what causes asthma. What they do know is that heredity plays an important role. In fact, genes linked to asthma have been discovered. Most likely it is not just one asthma gene at fault, but rather a combination of genes. These genes can be passed from one generation to the next. A person who inherits this unlucky combination does not actually inherit the disease, but rather a *tendency* to develop it. Kids with a family history of asthma have a greater chance of developing the disease than those with no family history of asthma. For example, if one parent has asthma, there is a 40 to 50 percent chance that the child will develop the disease. If both parents have asthma, the risk increases to 80 percent or more.[2]

Heredity is not the whole story. Even if a person does inherit these genes, it does not guarantee that he or she will develop asthma. Also, sometimes people develop asthma even though neither parent has it. Scientists say that environment, then, is also important. Whether or not a person develops the disease may depend on both heredity and environmental factors. In other words, asthma may be the result of being born

Twin Studies

Researchers have done a number of studies on twins to show the importance of both heredity and environment in the development of asthma. In 1995, for example, a study was conducted on 325 pairs of twins, including 94 pairs in which at least one twin had asthma. Of these, 39 pairs were identical twins (sharing the exact same genes), and 55 pairs were fraternal (with different genes). In 23 of the 39 pairs of identical twins, both twins had asthma—a 59 percent rate. In 13 of the 55 pairs of fraternal twins, both twins had asthma—only 24 percent. If asthma were determined only by genes, then the rate among the identical twins should have been 100 percent (since they share the same genes). The 59 percent result shows that environmental factors must also be involved.[3]

with twitchy lungs and then being exposed to irritating substances, such as smoke or dust.

What Role Does Allergy Play?

We know that most people with asthma also have allergies. And like asthma, allergies have a genetic link. People with allergies are born with a tendency to overreact to substances that are normally harmless. For example, most people can breathe the summer air or play with a cat without sneezing. But for people with allergies, these kinds of things may trigger an asthma attack. Many people with allergies do not develop asthma. But having allergies can increase the chances of developing the disease.

What happens during an allergy attack? Usually you get sick when germs enter your body. The body has many defenses against germs. The body's defenders, the white blood cells, are called in to fight these foreign invaders and protect you from further harm. The white blood cells are jelly-like blobs that can swim easily through blood and squeeze between body cells. They are part of the immune system.

Some white blood cells go after the germs and gobble them up. Others make special proteins called antibodies, which may damage the germs or make them easier to kill. The antibodies that fight germs are called immunoglobulin Gs (IgGs).

After the battle is over, some of the antibodies stay in the body. If the same kind of germs invade again, the cells can copy the antibodies quickly, making a whole new supply to fight the germs. As a result, the person will not get sick. The person has become immune to that illness.

People with allergies have an immune system that is a little too active. It makes antibodies against chemicals that would not have caused any harm. A substance that causes an allergic reaction is called an allergen. These may be chemicals on the surface of dust or pollen grains, or chemicals in foods. Pollen is a very common trigger for people with asthma. Many people who have seasonal asthma have attacks during the "hay fever season." Other allergenic triggers, such as house dust and molds, are around all year. They can be found throughout the house, in mattresses, in closets, in carpets, or on stuffed animals. During an allergic reaction, the body produces antibodies called immunglobulin Es (IgEs).

Many people with allergies do not develop asthma. But having allergies can increase the chances of developing the disease.

IgEs can be found in various parts of the body—the nose, throat, lungs, stomach, and skin. These antibodies are Y-shaped. The arms of the Y can latch onto allergens. Different IgEs match different kinds of allergens, latching onto them the way a key fits into a lock. For example, a mold allergen fits perfectly with one kind of

IgE, while a grass pollen allergen fits together with another type of IgE.

The "foot" of the IgE's Y-shape can attach to special body cells called mast cells. They are found in the same places as the IgEs—the skin, the lining of the nose, the throat, the stomach, and the lungs. Trouble starts when IgEs that are attached to mast cells grab hold of allergens. The mast cells then send out chemicals, including one called histamine. Histamine's job is to help fight invaders. It produces inflammation, making body cells swollen and watery. That is why your nose and eyes may start to run when you breathe in pollen grains, dust, or molds. White blood cells can move more easily in inflamed cells. When real germs are invading, inflammation is a good thing. But a reaction to a harmless allergen just makes a person feel miserable.

If you have an allergy, the first time you are exposed to the allergen, you may not have any allergy symptoms at all. For example, if you breathe in cat dander, your body may mistake it for an invader and produce IgE, but there may not be enough of the antibodies to bother you.

The next time you are exposed to cat dander, your body produces more IgEs. As you continue to spend

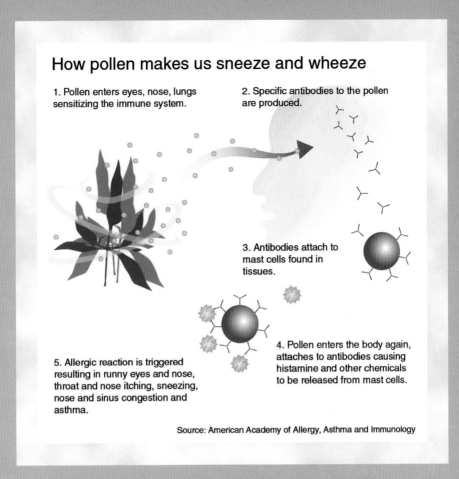

How pollen makes us sneeze and wheeze

1. Pollen enters eyes, nose, lungs sensitizing the immune system.

2. Specific antibodies to the pollen are produced.

3. Antibodies attach to mast cells found in tissues.

4. Pollen enters the body again, attaches to antibodies causing histamine and other chemicals to be released from mast cells.

5. Allergic reaction is triggered resulting in runny eyes and nose, throat and nose itching, sneezing, nose and sinus congestion and asthma.

Source: American Academy of Allergy, Asthma and Immunology

The body makes antibodies every time it is exposed to an allergen. It may take a long time before enough antibodies are made to cause an allergic reaction.

time around cats, your body reacts even more. This kind of exposure buildup is called sensitization. Finally your body becomes so sensitive to cat dander that you will have an allergic reaction, such as sneezing or coughing, every time you are near a cat. This process may not happen all in one day. It can take weeks, months, or even years to develop an allergy.

Olympic swimmer Nancy Hogshead (far right) showed her first symptoms of asthma during the 1984 Olympics at the age of twenty-two. Since then she has learned to take her asthma seriously to prevent a potentially dangerous attack.

5

Diagnosing and Treating Asthma

At just fourteen years old, Nancy Hogshead earned the top spot at the international swimming competition, ranking her the best swimmer in the world. Her dream was to make it to the Olympics. She trained hard and made the American team for the 1980 Olympics. But the U.S. boycotted the Olympics that year, and with great disappointment, Nancy had to stay home.

Through high school and college, Nancy broke a number of school records at swim meets. At the age of twenty-two, she not only made it to the 1984 Olympics, she won four medals—three gold and one silver. While competing for a fifth medal, Nancy had trouble catching her breath. An Olympic physician saw her coughing and told her that she needed medical treatment right away.

Nancy could not imagine what could be wrong. She was an Olympic gold-medal winner. She was strong and healthy, she thought. When she visited a doctor, Nancy was shocked to find out that she had asthma. "I thought people with asthma were sickly wheezers. I was a world-champion swimmer, hardly a weakling. Sure, I was sick a lot and tended to cough during and after working out, but who doesn't breathe hard after an intense match against worthy opponents?" The doctor told Nancy that people with asthma do not always wheeze (which she did not). Even more interesting, she learned, was that about 10 percent of Olympic athletes all over the world have asthma.

> About 10 percent of Olympic athletes all over the world have asthma.

The doctor asked Nancy to do a number of asthma tests. She had to run on a treadmill so that the doctor could observe the effects asthma had on her while she exercised. She also had to breathe into a peak flow meter, a device that measures how fast air flows out of the lungs. Nancy could not believe that sometimes her lungs were taking in 40 percent less air than usual. It was amazing she was able to swim!

To treat the breathlessness she felt during exercise, Nancy was prescribed a bronchodilator. This drug widens the airways by relaxing the muscles of the bronchial tubes. She was thrilled about the idea of exercising without coughing or gasping for air. However, she did not realize the importance of managing her asthma properly. Often she waited too long before treating the symptoms, thinking they would go away. As a result, Nancy ended up in the hospital with a serious asthma attack. It was a scary, miserable experience, she recalled. She was angry and frustrated with herself because she did not manage her condition the way the doctor had explained to her.

From then on, Nancy made asthma management part of her daily routine. In order to get her asthma under control, she needed to treat her symptoms right away, no matter how mild—even if she thought she could handle it. She learned how to pick up the warning signs that an attack was coming on. She even learned how to predict an attack when her peak flow reading was too low. She also figured out which medicines worked better than others. It took about a year, but

Nancy finally managed to take hold of her asthma instead of the other way around. Nancy wants other people to learn from her experience, and says: "Having asthma is no reason to be sick. It may take a while, but if you work with your doctor, you'll find the best way to treat your asthma!"[1]

Going to the Doctor

How do you know if you should see a doctor? If you get sick a lot, or you have a "cold" that doesn't seem to go away, it is usually a good idea to get it checked out. For some people with asthma, the signs may be obvious—wheezing, shortness of breath. Wheezing may be the most typical sign of asthma, but not everybody with asthma wheezes. Coughing is actually much more common, but it can also be a sign of other respiratory conditions, including the common cold or the flu. Asthma symptoms are also different in different people, and they may be mild or very serious. Some kids have asthma symptoms at night and then feel fine during the day. All these things make it hard to identify the condition. Yet it is important to diagnose asthma as soon as possible so that effective treatment can begin right away.

To diagnose asthma, a doctor will need to ask you

some questions about the illness and your family's medical history. Does anyone in your family have asthma or allergies? When did the breathing problems begin? What are the symptoms? How serious are they? When and where do they occur? How long do they last? Does the problem get worse after crying, laughing, or exercising? Are you exposed to cigarette smoke, air pollution, or other irritants?

Can Kids Outgrow Asthma?

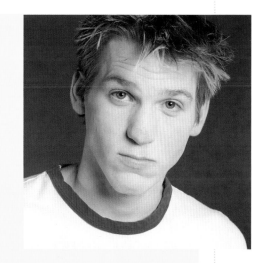

Many people think that kids outgrow asthma. This belief is not exactly true. For some kids, asthma symptoms seem to get worse over time. In others, the condition seems to get better as they get older. This may be partly due to the rapid growth spurt a child experiences during puberty.

As the body grows, so do the airways, and their larger diameter makes breathing easier. Studies have found that about half of the kids diagnosed with asthma at a young age seem to "outgrow" it by their teen years. However, this effect may not be long-lasting—the asthma symptoms may return later in life.

Testing Your Breathing

After asking questions, the doctor will give you a physical exam, starting with your nose, to look for signs of allergy or upper respiratory infection. He or she will then use a stethoscope to listen to your heart and lungs. If you are not having any symptoms at the moment, your breathing will probably sound normal. Sometimes, if you are having serious breathing problems, the doctor may use a chest X-ray to see if the airways are blocked.

The doctor may use special breathing tests to confirm an asthma diagnosis. One common breathing test is called spirometry (*spiro* comes from the Latin word meaning to breathe). During the test, the patient takes a deep breath, then exhales forcefully into a mouthpiece attached to a spirometer. This device measures how much and how quickly air flows in and out of the lungs when a person breathes. If the airways are wide open, air can flow quickly. If the airways are narrowed due to an asthma reaction, then the air flows slowly. However, airways may be narrowed for reasons other than asthma, such as a respiratory infection or exposure to cigarette smoke. Therefore, the patient may be given quick-acting asthma medication, which opens up airways. If the spirometer shows that the airflow greatly improves within five to ten minutes, then this is more evidence that the person has asthma.

There is one testing device that patients can use in their own homes—the peak flow meter. This device measures how fast air flows out of the lungs when a person exhales quickly. If the peak flow meter shows a drop in airflow, this could be a sign that an asthma attack is developing, even before the person is noticing breathing problems. This can help asthma patients treat the symptoms early, before they have a chance to get worse.

The peak flow meter measures the speed of air being exhaled. It allows asthma patients to know when an asthma attack may be developing, before they begin feeling any symptoms.

Testing for Allergies

Since allergens are some of the most common triggers of asthma, allergy testing is an important tool for diagnosis. Skin testing is used to identify the allergens that may be causing the person's asthma attacks. Allergens are placed on skin that is scratched or pricked with a plastic needle. Sometimes small amounts of an allergen solution are injected into the skin. If the skin becomes red and swollen within fifteen minutes, the person is sensitive to that allergen.

> A doctor may use special breathing tests to confirm an asthma diagnosis. One test is called spirometry. Another is a peak flow test.

There are also blood tests used to determine allergies. One test, RAST, measures amounts of IgEs in the blood that are caused by specific allergens. For example, a person who has IgEs for dust mites in his or her blood is probably allergic to dust mites.

Doctors usually use skin tests rather than RAST. Skin tests are generally more accurate, less expensive, and give immediate results. However, both of these tests tell us about *skin* reactions, not about an asthma reaction. Breathing in allergens is potentially dangerous, and waiting for reactions is time-consuming. However, it is believed that if allergens injected into the skin start a skin reaction, it is also likely that inhaled allergens cause a similar reaction in the bronchial tubes, making them narrow. Allergy tests are actually used to test for allergies, not asthma. But they can be used to identify the allergies that may be causing or worsening a person's asthma.

How Bad Is It?

Once a diagnosis is made, it is important to find out whether the asthma is mild, severe, or somewhere in between. This can help physicians determine the best treatment plan for the patient. Health experts have classified asthma into four main groups:

Mild intermittent asthma

- Symptoms occur generally less than twice a week.
- Nighttime symptoms occur less than twice a month.
- Asthma episodes are brief (lasting less than an hour) and do not occur very often.
- Lung function is normal between flare-ups.
- People may have severe attacks.

Mild persistent asthma

- Symptoms occur more than twice a week, but not every day.

- Nighttime symptoms occur more than twice a month (but less than every week).

- Episodes may affect activity.

- Lung function is normal between flare-ups.

Moderate persistent asthma

- Symptoms occur every day.

- Nighttime symptoms occur more than once a week.

- A quick-acting bronchodilator is used every day.

- Episodes may affect activity.

- Episodes occur more than two times a week and may last for days.

- Lung function is below normal, even between episodes.

Severe persistent asthma

- Symptoms occur throughout the day on most days.

- Nighttime symptoms occur nearly every night.

- Episodes limit activity.

- Episodes occur several times a day.

- Quick-acting medicine is needed frequently.

- Lung function is below normal, even between episodes.

How Is Asthma Treated?

There is no cure for asthma, but it can be controlled. Asthma patients need to work closely with their doctors to figure out an action plan that works best for them. An action plan explains what medications should be taken and other things the person needs to do to keep the asthma under control, such as avoiding triggers. Each person with asthma has different needs, so every action plan is different. With an effective plan, people with asthma can live normal lives.

Asthma can be treated with asthma medication. Medication comes in many forms, including pills, liquids, and injections, but the inhaler is the most popular device people use for asthma treatment. It is fast, easy, and handy. This handheld device turns liquid asthma medicine into a fine mist or powder that is inhaled into the lungs. The drug works right there to open up the airways and relieve the symptoms. Young children may be unable to use an inhaler, and may need to use another device, called a nebulizer. A nebulizer is an electric or

> There is no cure for asthma, but it can be controlled. Asthma patients need to work closely with their doctors to figure out an action plan that works best for them.

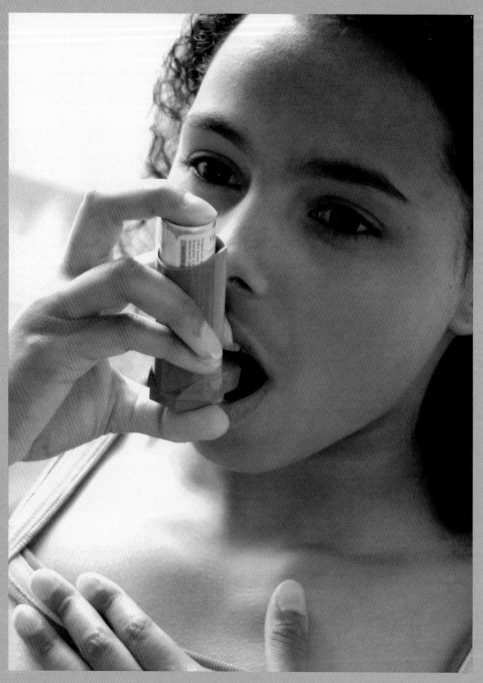

Many asthma patients carry an inhaler for fast relief from asthma symptoms. The medicine in the inhaler is taken directly into the lungs to open up the airways and make breathing easier.

battery-operated machine, which, like an inhaler, creates a mist of medicine that is breathed into the lungs. The child breathes through a mouthpiece or a face mask. Nebulizers are not as convenient as inhalers, and they take five to ten minutes to deliver medication.

There are two main types of medicines: quick-relief and long-term control.

Asthma can be treated with asthma medication. Medication comes in many forms, including pills, liquids, and injections, but the inhaler is the most popular device people use for asthma treatment.

A popular quick-relief medicine is a short-acting bronchodilator. Bronchodilators are drugs that work by relaxing the muscles in the airways, allowing the narrowed airways to open up. Then air can flow in and out more easily, making it easier to breathe. They are usually given through an inhaler or a nebulizer. Short-acting bronchodilators work quickly and are sometimes called "rescue" or "relief" medicines. They can be taken at the first sign of an attack and relieve or stop symptoms within minutes. If the person needs to use a short-acting bronchodilator more than twice a week to stop asthma attacks, the asthma is not

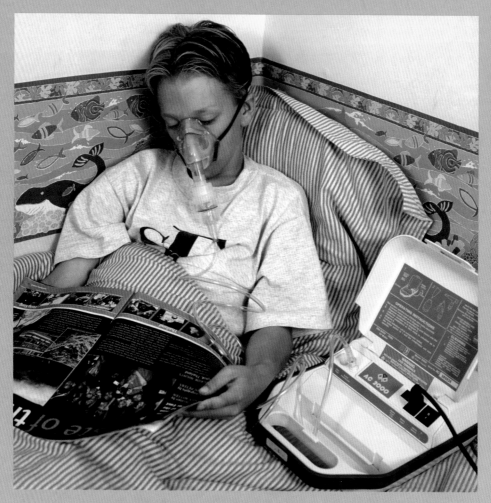

Some children find it easier to receive their asthma medication through an electronic machine called a nebulizer. They breathe their medication through a face mask. Nebulizers are also used for emergency treatment of asthma attacks.

under good control. The doctor may need to prescribe long-term control medicines.

Long-term control medicines, sometimes called controller medications, can actually *prevent* asthma attacks. They need to be taken regularly, once or twice a day. Regular use of these drugs can help make the airways less sensitive and less likely to start a reaction. The controller medicines most commonly used are anti-inflammatory drugs. Many health experts believe that it is most important to treat the main problem of asthma—inflammation of the airways. Anti-inflammatory

Aren't Steroids Bad?

You have probably heard about some sports stars who take steroids. Those steroids are drugs that are used to build up muscles. But those drugs are dangerous and illegal. The steroids used to treat asthma are not the same as the illegal steroids. They are anti-inflammatory drugs. When they are taken in the right amounts under a doctor's supervision, they are safe and effective. In fact, they are a real lifesaver. They help to reduce inflammation in a person's airways during an asthma attack, allowing them to breathe easier again.

drugs can do the job by reducing the swelling and twitchiness in the airways. They can be given through an inhaler or nebulizer, or swallowed in a pill or liquid form. The most effective anti-inflammatory drugs used to treat asthma are called steroids. These drugs are safe when taken as directed by the patient's doctor.

Long-acting bronchodilators may also be used for long-term control. They are not anti-inflammatory drugs. They work in the same way as short-acting bronchodilators, but take an hour or more to take effect. One treatment is good for up to twelve hours and can actually prevent asthma attacks. They cannot be used for quick relief, however, because they do not work fast enough. They should not be used *instead of* anti-inflammatory drugs—they could cover up the signs that the asthma is getting worse and lead to more severe attacks.

Asthma attacks that are caused by allergens can be controlled with medications that treat allergy symptoms. Many people take antihistamines. Remember, histamine is the chemical that is released when the body is exposed to an allergen. It is the main cause of allergy symptoms. An antihistamine stops the effects of histamine. Nasal decongestants can also help to relieve allergy symptoms. These drugs reduce swelling in the nasal passages and widen the airways. They help to clear a stopped-up nose so that a person can breathe more easily.

Mast cell stabilizers are also used to treat allergies. These are drugs that work by stopping the mast cells

> Asthma attacks that are caused by allergens can be controlled with medications that treat allergy symptoms.

from reacting to allergens. When mast cells cannot release histamine, inflammation does not develop. These drugs need to be taken two to four times every day, and they can take up to four weeks to start working. They may help some people with exercise-induced asthma.

In 2003, the drug Xolair (omalizumab) was approved for a new type of treatment, called anti-IgE. This treatment is used for patients with allergies and moderate to severe asthma that is not successfully controlled by steroids. It works by blocking IgEs, the antibodies that react with allergens. The blocked IgEs cannot attach to allergens that enter the body, and thus an allergic reaction is prevented. Xolair is given by injection once or twice a month. This is a long-term control medicine, not for quick relief. Patients who take it usually have fewer episodes and need less steroids to keep their asthma under control.

What type of asthma medication do you need, and how much? That depends on how severe the symptoms are and how often they occur. People with mild asthma may just need fast-acting drugs that treat the symptoms on the spot.

People with a more serious case may need a long-term treatment plan. They may need to take medications every day to control inflammation and symptoms. Eventually, the person will have fewer attacks. The person should continue to take medication, however, to keep the symptoms from coming back.

Asthma treatment plans may include a combination of both fast-acting and long-term medicines. Finding the right treatment can be a long process, but the key to control is consistently following the doctor's plan. There may be a temptation to stop taking the medications once symptoms have improved. This should not be done, however, without the doctor's approval.

6

Preventing Asthma Attacks

In 2000, John was only six years old when he had a severe asthma attack, right after soccer practice at his school in Springfield, Missouri. He was rushed to the hospital and hooked up to a ventilator, a machine to help him breathe. John was also given powerful medication to treat his asthma. After four days, he was well enough to go home.

Two weeks later, John had another really bad asthma attack. This time he was flown to St. Louis Children's Hospital, where his family was told that his disease was severe. If they did not come up with an effective treatment plan for his asthma soon, he could die.

John's parents decided to sign John up for a special program for managing asthma, created by Dr. Robert Strunk at the St. Louis hospital. In this program, asthma patients work closely with doctors and nurses to develop an action plan. The plan will contain guidelines to manage symptoms, as well as information on what to do when the asthma starts to get out of control. Their focus is on prevention. Managing asthma means stopping the attacks *before* they happen. Patients and their families are taught to watch for early warning signs of an attack. They learn how to use "rescue medication" to keep

Dr. Robert Strunk works with asthma patients at the St. Louis Children's Hospital. He teaches them to take measures that will prevent asthma attacks before they happen.

the problem from getting worse and thus avoid a trip to the hospital. They also learn how important it is to take anti-inflammatory medication every day, even when the person is feeling perfectly fine.

Another important part of the plan is to identify the asthma triggers and then avoid them. John was tested for a number of allergens. The test results showed he was allergic to dust mites, pollens, animal dander, milk, eggs, and peanuts. "We have protective coverings on the bed, an air filter, and no pets," John's mother commented. "We had to give away our dog," a loss she said was a small price to pay for a healthier child. She also talked to John's school about his condition. His classroom is air-conditioned, and the school nurse knows all about his treatments.

> Managing asthma means stopping the attacks *before* they happen.

Now John is a healthy, active kid who loves to play sports. Every morning, he checks his breathing by blowing into his peak flow meter. He can identify the first signs of trouble, and he takes his medication every day. "With medication and strict monitoring," his mother said, "he can lead a normal life."[1]

Avoiding the Triggers

The best way to be asthma-free, or at least to reduce the risk of asthma attacks, is to avoid the triggers. This can be done in a number of ways:

Dust mites. Probably the hardest allergen to get rid of is house dust. Dust and the mites that live in it are everywhere—on carpets, bookshelves, curtains, stuffed toys. These things should be taken out of the person's bedroom. The room should be cleaned at least twice a week to keep dust from building up. Mattresses and pillows are also dust collectors. Placing them in dust-proof covers can help. Bedding should be washed in hot water once a week.

Pollens. If the allergies are seasonal—they occur at certain times of the year—the person should try to stay indoors during those times. This is especially helpful in the middle of the day, when the pollen counts are usually highest. Keep the windows closed so that the pollen does not get into the house. Use air-conditioning instead. An air cleaner with a HEPA filter (high-efficiency particulate air filter) takes allergens out of the air, so it can help reduce allergens in the house.

Molds. Molds can be a problem. Like pollen, they can travel through the air and enter the house through open windows. Molds multiply quickly in any damp environment, especially in the bathroom. Chlorine is a very effective mold killer. It will get rid of molds growing on shower curtains and bathroom tiles. A dehumidifier can help to keep the house dry.

Animal dander. Giving up a pet can be very difficult for people with asthma. They may not want to do it, even if the pet causes them a severe reaction. It might be helpful to keep the pet out of the bedroom and always keep the door closed. But some people with asthma are so sensitive that they could have a reaction even when the animal is in another room. The problem with pets is that their dander usually drifts throughout the house. It is a good idea to remove the pet—either give it away or keep it outside—and then clean the house thoroughly. (It can take months before all the animal dander is gone.)

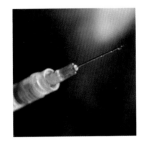

Colds and flu. Colds and flu are common triggers of asthma attacks, especially

Dr. Platts-Mills

SPOTLIGHT
Can You Keep Your Cats?

"Get rid of your pets!" For years, that was the standard advice that doctors gave patients who had just been diagnosed with asthma. But that may not be necessary, according to studies headed by Dr. Thomas Platts-Mills, a researcher at the University of Virginia. Dr. Platts-Mills has been studying common household allergens that can trigger asthma attacks. The most common sources are dust mites, cats, and cockroaches. In studies of dust mite and cockroach allergens, Dr. Platts-Mills and his associates found that the higher the amount of allergen in the air, the more likely children will become allergic to it and develop asthma. But cat allergens do not seem to work that way.

Measuring the amount of cat allergen in the homes of more than two hundred children and testing the children for asthma, the researchers found that low to moderate amounts of cat allergen did result in allergies. But growing up in a house with high

among children. It is important for people with asthma to stay away from anyone who has a cold. Flu, or influenza, is a very contagious, serious viral infection that affects the whole body, especially the lungs. To prevent flu, doctors often recommend getting flu shots. However, people who are allergic to eggs should not get amounts of cat allergen actually seemed to protect children from allergies. They had less of the IgE "allergy antibodies" and were less likely to have asthma than children who grew up in houses without pets. Blood tests showed that exposure to cats seemed to work in much the same way as allergy shots. The children's bodies formed protective antibodies that blocked the IgE reaction.

"This result alters the advice we give patients," Dr. Platts-Mills says. "I would not recommend that all parents get rid of their cat because they are concerned their child might develop asthma." Since high exposure to cat allergen is protective for some children, he comments that there is no need to get rid of a pet unless the child is wheezing and has a positive skin test to cat allergen.[2]

Dr. Platts-Mills is also studying patients whose asthma is not caused by a reaction to inhaled allergens. He has found evidence that common fungi, such as the athlete's foot fungus, may play an important role in this kind of asthma. He suggests that if this is so, these patients could be treated with antifungal drugs.[3]

a flu shot. Although new vaccines are being developed, the flu vaccine used by flu shot clinics is grown in chicken eggs and can cause a serious reaction in an egg-sensitive asthma patient.

It is also a good idea to get a vaccination against pneumococcal pneumonia, a serious lung infection caused by bacteria. Pneumonia can be very dangerous for anyone, but especially for people with asthma.

Food allergies. Food allergy is a trigger for some asthma patients. It makes sense to remove the specific food from the diet. If it is not clear which food is causing trouble, keeping a food diary could help. It should include all foods and drinks consumed, as well as any asthma symptoms that develop. Going over these daily records, in consultation with a doctor, may reveal which foods are asthma triggers.

Irritants. Cigarette smoke is a big problem for people with asthma. When a person breathes in cigarette smoke, the harmful chemicals in it—such as carbon monoxide—go right into the lungs.

Carbon monoxide is very dangerous because it keeps the blood from bringing oxygen to the brain, heart, lungs, and other important organs in the body. Cigarette smoke also damages the cilia in the lining of the airways. Eventually, the cilia are unable to sweep mucus and foreign particles out of the lungs and up toward the throat. Some chemicals in cigarette smoke stay in the lungs. They can cause some serious illnesses, such as bronchitis, emphysema, and lung cancer. If these things can happen to a person with healthy lungs, can you imagine what smoking can do to someone with asthma?

It is hard to avoid air pollution. Although soot particles and other irritants in the air are produced mainly in cities, they are carried all over the world by the atmosphere. But there are some ways people with asthma can protect themselves from these triggers. Checking the local Air Quality Index is a good first step.

Secondhand Smoke

Studies have shown that smoking is bad not only for the smoker, it is also harmful to anyone around that person. Secondhand smoke—the smoke that people around a smoker breathe—can be very dangerous to someone with asthma. Smokers who have children with asthma should never smoke around their children. Even smoking in the same house can leave harmful chemicals that can linger for hours. According to the Centers for Disease Control and Prevention, each year as many as 26,000 new cases of asthma in children may be caused by parents who smoke in the home.[4]

Weather reports on TV and radio usually give the AQI, and it can also be found in newspapers and on Web sites such as AIRNow, at <http://airnow.gov>. Staying indoors or taking it easier while working or playing outdoors when the AQI is "unhealthy" can help protect sensitive lungs. Air conditioners can help keep indoor air healthy during the summer. They not only cool air and remove moisture but also filter out dust and irritating particles. Air cleaning machines can help all year round. Health experts say that those with a HEPA filter are the most effective.

Exercise. Exercise may be a common trigger for people with asthma, but it should not be avoided. Instead, it should be managed with the help of a doctor's advice. Exercise is actually very important  because it can help keep the body healthy. It helps to strengthen the heart and lungs, which is especially important for people with asthma. A person whose body is physically fit is more capable of handling an asthma attack. Exercise can also help a person feel good about him- or herself. A good attitude is very important, since many people with exercise-induced bronchospasm (EIB) link exercise with an attack.

People with asthma can do any kind of exercise, including jogging, dancing, bike riding, weight lifting, and swimming. Doctors often recommend swimming because the air near pools is usually warm and moist. (Remember cold, dry air may trigger an attack.)

> The best way to be asthma-free, or at least to reduce the risk of asthma attacks, is to avoid the triggers.

Whatever the exercise, it needs to be something that the person enjoys and will continue doing.

Olympic athletes with asthma say that it is important to do warm-ups before exercising. This helps the muscles to warm up gradually and reduces the risk of an EIB. Asthma medication may be taken before exercising to prevent an asthma attack, if advised by a doctor as part of the action plan.

Getting Allergies Under Control

Since most people with asthma have allergy triggers, one way to avoid an allergic reaction is by getting allergy shots. Doctors call this immunotherapy. The idea is to make the body less sensitive to the allergens that cause a reaction. That way the immune system doesn't identify them as foreign and attack them. Each shot contains a tiny amount of an allergen. When it is injected below the skin, some of the allergen gets into the blood and causes the body to make antibodies for

> Exercise may be a common trigger for people with asthma, but it should not be avoided. Exercise is actually very important because it can help keep the body healthy.

that allergen. These new antibodies are different from the ones that the body makes in allergy reactions. They react with the allergen and block it from reacting with allergy antibodies. They also reeducate the immune system so that it learns to react more normally.

Each successive injection contains a little more of the allergen, and more blocking antibodies are made. After a while, there is enough of the blocking antibody to tie up the allergen and keep it from causing trouble. The body is now desensitized, and the allergen no longer triggers an allergic reaction. People need to have allergy shots regularly for the treatment to be effective. The shots may be given once a week at first, and then gradually reduced to once a month. Usually people have to continue the allergy shots for years to avoid future allergic reactions.

How's Your Peak Flow?

You can get an idea on how well your asthma is doing by checking your peak flow. Remember, a peak flow meter is a device that measures air flowing out of the lungs. It can show when the airways are narrowing *before* asthma symptoms develop. This device is used mainly by people with moderate to severe and persistent asthma. It can let people know a number of important things:

- when emergency treatment is needed
- how well the asthma is being managed and controlled
- when to stop or add medication, as directed by a doctor
- what triggers the asthma attack (such as exercise-induced bronchospasm)

Not everyone needs to use a peak flow meter every day. The doctor will determine whether or not a person needs to use one. However, people who have to take medicine every day may need to use a peak flow meter once or twice a day to see if the medicine is working the way it is supposed to.

Once you are ready to use a peak flow meter, you need to find out your personal best peak flow rate. This number is different for everybody. A "personal best" is the peak flow rate a person has when the asthma is under control. To get this number, you have to take a reading twice a day (morning and night) for at least two weeks. The personal best is your goal number. You may not get the same reading in the future, but you should try to get as close to it as possible.

> People with asthma can learn to identify the early warning signs of an asthma attack. Treating the condition before it has a chance to get worse can help to keep the asthma under control.

Early Warning Signs

People with asthma can learn to identify the early warning signs of an asthma attack. Treating the condition before it has a chance to get worse can help to keep

Green Is for GO!

The numbers on a peak flow meter fall into three color zones: green, yellow, and red, just like a traffic light. These zones are set up by a health-care provider and correspond to the color zones in the action plan.

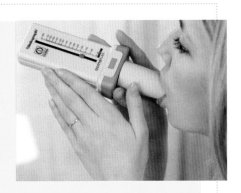

Each color zone shows how well you are doing:

- Green zone means "GO." Peak flow rates are 80 to 100 percent of your personal best. Air flow is normal. There are no symptoms during the day or night. You can do your usual activities and take your medicines as usual.

- Yellow zone means "CAUTION" or "SLOW DOWN." Peak flow rates are 50 to 80 percent of your personal best. The airways are starting to narrow. Mild symptoms may develop, including coughing, wheezing, or chest tightness. You may have difficulty doing some everyday activities. Symptoms may interrupt sleeping. You may be having an asthma episode and need to take more medicine. Or your doctor may need to change your action plan.

- Red zone means "STOP" or "DANGER." Peak flow rates are less than 50 percent of your personal best. This reading indicates a medical emergency. The airways are seriously narrowed. Symptoms may include persistent coughing, shortness of breath, and wheezing. You may have trouble walking and talking. You are unable to do normal activities. Call your doctor right away if quick-relief medicines do not bring your peak flow number back into the yellow or green zone.[5]

the asthma under control. Here are some clues that an
attack may be coming on:

- coughing
- tightness in the chest
- throat clearing
- fast or unusual breathing
- inability to stand still or sit still
- extreme tiredness
- restless sleep

The Asthma Control Test™ is a quick and easy way
to find out if your asthma is under control. You can find
it at <http://www.asthmacontrol.com>.

7

Asthma and the Future

Doctors have long known that when air pollution is high, hospital admissions for asthma go up. This is especially obvious in places like Sacramento, California, where ozone levels often rise into the "unhealthy" range. Researchers at the University of California, Davis (UC Davis) in Sacramento have been studying the effects of ozone exposure on the lungs of rhesus monkeys. They chose these animals because their lungs, like those of humans, continue to develop after birth. In the UC Davis experiments, monkeys were exposed to ozone in a pattern similar to the weather in the Sacramento area. They breathed air contaminated with ozone for five days, then normal air for nine days. This cycle was repeated for five months. The amounts of ozone in the air were three times as high as those on smog-alert days in Los Angeles. They were similar to ozone levels on an average day in Mexico City.

When baby monkeys were exposed to ozone soon after birth, their lungs did not develop normally. There were fewer branches from the bronchi, and there were other changes in lung structure similar to those in human asthma patients. The airways also became hyperreactive (twitchy). Changes of the lungs were even greater in the experimental monkeys that had been exposed to house dust mite allergens in addition to the ozone. When these young monkeys later breathed air containing the allergen, their breathing became rapid and shallow, and there was less oxygen in their blood. These reactions were very similar to an asthma episode in humans. It seemed that ozone not only triggered an asthma reaction, but also helped to cause the condition. "We have the first real monkey model of human asthma here," remarked UC Davis researcher Dallas Hyde. "What we are seeing is quite disturbing, as we would not have assumed these levels (of ozone) would change lung development." These animal studies support the

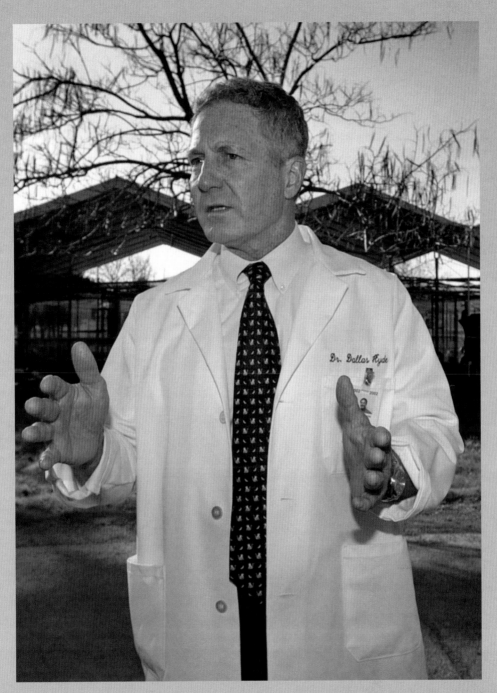

Dr. Dallas Hyde has done research on the development of lungs in baby monkeys at the University of California, Davis. He found that exposure to ozone increased the risk of asthma development.

findings of a survey of freshmen at UC Berkeley: Students who had grown up in counties with high ozone levels were more likely to have asthma.[1]

Cleaning the Air

A number of laws, including the Clean Air Act of 1990 and various local regulations, have already done a lot to reduce air pollution in the United States. Similar measures are being taken in other countries of the world. But a lot still remains to be done. Environmental Defense, a nonprofit organization, has proposed three steps for "pollution solutions":[2]

1. Clean smokestacks. That black smoke that puffs out of factory smokestacks contains more than just soot. Smokestacks send nitrogen oxides, sulfur dioxide, and other dangerous pollutants into the air, which also add to ozone pollution. In 2005, the Environmental Protection Agency (EPA) proposed the Clean Air Interstate Rule (CAIR), a program to reduce smokestack pollution by 80 percent over a period of ten years.[3]

2. Clean tailpipes. Car and truck exhausts are another big source of harmful air pollution. The soot particles produced by diesel engines in trucks, ships, railroad locomotives, pumps, and generators are especially dangerous for people with asthma. The EPA has set strong standards for new diesel engines in trucks, but most of the trucks on the

Exhaust from cars and trucks pollute the air. People who live near highways breathe in more pollution and have greater risk of developing asthma than if they lived somewhere less crowded.

road have old engines that do not meet these standards. It will be decades before the new emission standards have a major effect. However, some companies are working to put cleaner trucks on the road. In 2004, for example, FedEx put sixteen new diesel-electric delivery trucks into service in Sacramento, New York, and Tampa. These new trucks produce 90 percent less emissions, and they are cheaper to run.[4]

3. Reduce exposure to traffic pollution. Studies have shown that children who live near highways with heavy traffic have more asthma and other lung problems than those who live in less crowded areas. Today's cars and trucks have much cleaner emissions than those of the 1980s, but there are a lot more of them. To reduce air pollution in cities, says Environmental Defense, we need to promote more use of public transportation systems. We need to manage traffic growth and design neighborhoods where people can walk to shopping and entertainment instead of driving cars.[5]

Toward Better Treatments

There are very good drugs available now for controlling asthma, preventing attacks, and stopping them when they do occur. But all of today's asthma drugs have unpleasant side effects, and they do not work equally well for everyone. A great deal of asthma research is aimed at discovering new and better treatments.

Much of this modern asthma research is focused on allergy-related asthma. Doctors are studying the basic steps in an allergic reaction and how such a reaction can trigger an asthma episode. Studies at Harvard Medical School, for example, are focused on one type of white blood cells that are especially active during allergic reactions. Drugs that interfere with the work of these

A Win for the Olympics

In the list of U.S. cities with the worst ozone pollution, Atlanta, Georgia, ranks in the top twenty-five. So when Atlanta hosted the Summer Olympics in 1996, the city made a special effort to cope with the heavy traffic. During the seventeen days the games were held, the downtown area was closed to private cars, and extra public transit was provided. City businesses were encouraged to have their workers do some of their work at home or shift their working hours to reduce crowding on the highways. These measures paid off. In spite of all the extra people visiting the city, the peak ozone levels each day dropped 28 percent—and there were nearly 20 percent fewer hospital admissions for asthma than usual.[6]

white cells might help in treating chronic asthma.[7] Researchers at other institutes are trying to develop ways to stop the immune system from reacting to allergens, or to develop protective reactions instead of allergic reactions.

All of the body's activities, including the reactions of the immune system, are ultimately controlled by genes, contained in the DNA in each cell. Researchers all over the world have been of many different groups internationally, about half of these genes have already been searching for genes involved in allergic reactions and

> There are very good drugs available now for controlling asthma, preventing attacks, and stopping them when they do occur.

the development of asthma. According to Professor William Cookson of Oxford University, "There are perhaps ten genes that have a significant effect on a person's susceptibility to asthma, and more with minor effects. . . . As a result of the work of many different groups internationally, about half of these genes have already been identified. . . . Even without knowing all the genes involved in asthma, our ideas about the causes of the disease are changing and we are seeing new ways to treat the illness."[8]

In 2005, researchers at Cincinnati Children's Hospital Medical Center reported that they had found eight groups of asthma genes—a total of 161 genes in all. Using this information, researchers may be able to develop treatments targeted to a patient's own genetic makeup. The gene patterns may also be useful for predicting asthma attacks.[9]

Meanwhile, researchers at Brigham and Women's Hospital in Boston have discovered a gene that doesn't cause asthma; it *protects* people from it. "If you have this protective form of the gene," says Dr. Craig Lilly, the head of the research team, "you have half the asthma risk." The gene interferes with the work of a key inflammation chemical. People with this gene may be sensitive to asthma triggers, but their airways do not narrow when they are exposed to the triggers. New drugs to treat asthma, which work by blocking this chemical, are now being tested in humans.[10]

Asthma Vaccines?

Safe and effective treatments to prevent and stop asthma attacks can save lives. But with today's treatments a person with asthma must keep taking medicine— perhaps for a lifetime. It would be even better to be able to prevent the development of asthma before it starts. An asthma vaccine might be the answer.

> Safe and effective treatments to prevent and stop asthma attacks can save lives. It would be even better to be able to prevent the development of asthma before it starts. An asthma vaccine might be the answer.

Several groups are already testing new asthma vaccines on humans. One, for example, is based on a soil bacterium. Although related to the germ that causes tuberculosis, this bacterium is harmless. "It is commonly found in household water taps," says researcher Ratko Djukanovic at the University of Southampton, United Kingdom. His vaccine is based on the theory that our modern environment is too clean, and children's immune systems do not get enough practice fighting bacteria and viruses or learning to recognize ones that are harmless. The new vaccine is "a natural protector," which stimulates immune cells that stop the allergic reaction and restore the balance of the immune system.[11]

An asthma vaccine being tested in Singapore is based on a dust mite gene.[12] Another, developed at Dynavax Technologies in California, uses synthetic bacterial DNA to stimulate protection and stop allergic reactions. This vaccine cleared up the lungs of asthmatic rhesus monkeys. Tests in humans began in 2005. If they give similar results, this vaccine may not only prevent but actually reverse the development of asthma.[13]

The new vaccines probably will not be available before 2010. But vaccines such as these might be the cure that people with asthma have been waiting for.

Questions and Answers

A kid in my class has asthma. He sits right next to me. Sometimes he coughs a lot. Can I catch it from him? No. There are no asthma germs. People with asthma are born with sensitive lungs that overreact to things that don't normally cause trouble, such as dust or furry animals.

My little sister has asthma. Will she outgrow it? Probably not. For some kids with asthma, the disease seems to get better or disappear by the time they are teenagers. However, the asthma may return later in life.

Does having asthma mean you have to give up sports? No, not at all. In fact, many famous athletes have asthma. It is very important to make sure the asthma is under control first. Your doctor can advise you about medications you can take just before exercising to keep you from having an asthma episode. Staying active is important for everyone, and especially for people with asthma. Exercise helps to strengthen your lungs. Just don't exercise when pollution levels are high, or when other common allergy triggers are present.

My mom has asthma. Will I get it too? Not necessarily. But you are more likely to develop it than someone whose parents don't have asthma. It's a good idea to watch for any symptoms such as persistent coughing, wheezing, or difficulty breathing. Have a doctor check you if you notice any problems.

Aren't allergies and asthma basically the same thing? No. Allergies can trigger asthma symptoms, but the two conditions are not the same. An allergic reaction can make it difficult to breathe, but when the immune response calms down, the lungs work normally again. In asthma, the lungs are very sensitive (twitchy) and can react to nonallergenic triggers, too.

How can I tell if my asthma is getting out of control? There are some telltale signs to watch for. If you suddenly start getting symptoms at night, or if you need to use a bronchodilator for quick relief more than once or twice a week, you should see a doctor. Lower-than-usual peak flow readings can also be a warning sign. Your doctor may suggest changes in your treatment plan that will get your asthma back under control.

Would allergy shots help my asthma? That depends on whether you have allergies. You need to be tested first. Allergy shots may help to make you less sensitive to some allergens. In other cases, such as food allergies, it is easier just to avoid the allergen.

Asthma Timeline

1550 B.C.   Ebers Papyrus of ancient Egypt mentions treatment for asthma.

1000 B.C.   The ancient Chinese describe asthma in a medical textbook, suggesting using ma huang as treatment.

400 B.C.   Greek physician Hippocrates uses the term *asthma* to describe wheezing.

A.D. 200   Greek physician Galen describes clinical signs of asthma and recommends exposure to volcanic gases as a treatment.

Hippocrates

A.D. 600s   Greek physician Paul of Aegina uses drugs to clear airways of excess mucus.

1160   Jewish physician Maimonides suggests that asthma is hereditary.

1500s   Jerome Cardan notes a connection between asthma and allergies.

1698   Sir John Floyer publishes *A Treatise of the Asthma*, describing contraction of bronchial muscles.

1794   Dr. William Cullen complains about difficulties in diagnosing asthma because symptoms are similar to other respiratory illnesses.

1860	Henry Hyde Salter recommends strong black coffee to treat asthma.
1903	Adrenaline (epinephrine) is used in asthma treatment.
1924	Ma huang, used to treat asthma, makes it from China to the west.
1929	Adrenaline is first administered by an inhaler at Guy's Hospital in London.
1939	National Home for Jewish Children starts an asthma treatment program.
1940s	Dr. M. Murray Peshkin believes that asthma is caused by stress at home.
1951	Dr. Allan Hurst reports that changes in the immune system occur during an asthma attack.
1957	The National Home for Jewish Children sets up a new asthma research facility called the Children's Asthma Research Institute and Hospital.
1960s	Dr. Irving Itkin reports on the role of hyperreactive (twitchy) airways.
1966	Kimishige and Teruko Ishizaka discover the "allergy antibody" immunoglobulin E (IgE).

Kimishige and
Teruko Ishizaka

1970s Common triggers of asthma (allergens and others) are identified.

1991 National Institutes of Health guidelines stress the importance of controlling inflammation.

2003 FDA approves the first anti-IgE medication, Xolair (omalizumab).

2005 Cincinnati Children's Hospital Medical Center identifies eight groups of genes linked with asthma.

For More Information

Allergy and Asthma Network/Mothers of Asthmatics, Inc.
2751 Prosperity Avenue, Suite 150
Fairfax, VA 22031
Phone: 800-878-4403 or 703-641-9595
http://www.aanma.org

American Academy of Allergy, Asthma, and Immunology
555 East Wells Street, Suite 1100
Milwaukee, WI 53202-3823
Phone: 800-822-2762 or 414-272-6071
http://www.aaaai.org/

The American Lung Association
61 Broadway, 6th Floor
New York, NY 10006
Phone: 800-548-8252 or 212-315-8700
email: info@lungusa.org
http://www.lungusa.org

Asthma and Allergy Foundation of America
1233 20th Street, NW, Suite 402
Washington, DC 20036
Phone: 800-7-ASTHMA (800-727-8462)
  or 202-466-7643
email: info@aafa.org
http://www.aafa.org

National Heart, Lung, and Blood Institute
NHLBI Health Information Center
Attention: Web Site
P.O. Box 30105
Bethesda, MD 20824-0105
Phone: 301-592-8573
email: nhlbiinfo@nhlbi.nih.gov
http://www.nhlbi.nih.gov/health/public/
        lung/index.htm

National Jewish Medical and Research Center
1400 Jackson Street
Denver, CO 80206
Phone: 800-222-LUNG (5864)
email: lungline@njc.org
http://www.nationaljewish.org/

Chapter Notes

Chapter 1. Out of Breath

1. Wynonna Judd, "Waited to Exhale," *People Magazine*, November 4, 2002, pp. 115–117.

2. Ibid.

3. Evelyn B. Kelly, "Asthma: Biotech Is Bringing Forth New Products Against an Ancient Disease," *Modern Drug Discovery*, July 2004, p. 51.

4. Ibid.

5. Centers for Disease Control and Prevention, "Basic Facts about Asthma," reviewed February 10, 2005 <http://www.cdc.gov/asthma/faqs.htm> (February 17, 2005).

6. Dr. Stephen Redd, "Disease Detectives," Centers for Disease Control and Prevention, reviewed April 30, 2002, <http://www.bam.gov/sub_diseases/disease_detectives_1.html> (February 17, 2005).

7. Alica Bartz, "The Facts of Allergies & Asthma," *Mpls St. Paul Magazine*, April 2002, <http://www.mspmag.com/feature.asp?featureid=2855> (March 7, 2005).

Chapter 2. Asthma in History

1. Christopher Wagner, "Theodore Roosevelt: Childhood," December 5, 1999, revised January 20, 2003 <http://histclo.hispeed.com/pres/ind20/tr/tr-child.html> (February 21, 2005); Josh Cracraft, SparkNote on Theodore Roosevelt, revised March 25, 2005 <http://

www.sparknotes.com/biography/troosevelt/section1.
html> (April 3, 2005).

2. John Carpi, "Strategies: Huffing and Puffing."
Medical World News, September 1992, p. 19.

Chapter 3. What Is Asthma?

1. Gary Mihoces, "Bettis Learns How to Deal With
Asthma," *USA Today*, July 25, 2002, Sports section,
p. 2C.

2. Ibid.

3. James Gibbs, "Jerome Bettis Won't Be Stopped by
Asthma," August 18, 2003, <http://newpittsburghcourier.
com/?article=8577> (February 28, 2005).

4. Alica Bartz, "The Facts of Allergies & Asthma,"
Mpls St. Paul Magazine, April 2002, <http://www.
mspmag.com/feature.asp?featureid=2855> (March 7,
2005).

5. Energy Information Administration, Department
of Energy, "Mexico: Environmental Issues," January
2004, <http://www.eia.doe.gov/emeu/cabs/mexenv.
html> (March 27, 2005).

6. American Lung Association, "State of the Air:
2004," © 2004, <http://www.lungusa.org/site/pp.asp?c=
dvLUK9O0E&b=50752> (March 26, 2005).

7. American Lung Association, "Childhood Asthma
Overview," © 2004, <http://www.lungusa.org/site/pp.
asp?c=dvLUK9O0E&b=22782> (April 3, 2005).

Chapter 4. What Causes Asthma?

1. "Genetics of Asthma," *Discoveryhealth.com*,
July 16, 2000, <http://health.discovery.com/minisites/

dna/asthma.html> (February 24, 2005).

2. Frappa Stout, "What You Should Know About Asthma," *USA Weekend*, March 8–10, 2002, p. 10.

3. "Asthma and Genetics," December 9, 2002, <http://acc6.its.brooklyn.cuny.edu/~scintech/asthma/Genetics2.htm> (March 8, 2005).

Chapter 5. Diagnosing and Treating Asthma

1. Nancy Hogshead, "Personal Stories—Nancy Hogshead, 1984 Olympic Gold Medalist: Asthma," *Dr. Greene.com*, <http://www.drgreene.com/21_1339.html> (February 9, 2005).

Chapter 6. Preventing Asthma Attacks

1. Jane E. Brody, "Families Grab an Asthma Lifeline That Keeps Children Well and Active," *The New York Times*, October 28, 2003, p. F7.

2. National Institute of Allergy and Infectious Diseases, "Cats May Protect Against Asthma," *Asthma: Current NIAID Research Highlights*, March 2, 2005, <http://www2.niaid.nih.gov/newsroom/focuson/asthma01.research.htm> (March 11, 2005).

3. "Thomas A.E. Platts-Mills, M.D., Ph.D.," University of Virginia Health System, December 15, 2003 <http://www.healthsystem.virginia.edu/cic/faculty/plattsmills.cfm> (March 30, 2005).

4. Centers for Disease Control and Prevention, "Facts About Secondhand Smoke," reviewed January 26, 2005, <http://www.cdc.gov/tobacco/research_data/environmental/ets-fact.htm> (March 21, 2005).

5. "How To Use a Peak Flow Meter," Loyola University Stritch School of Medicine, February 20, 1996, <http://www.meddean.luc.edu/lumen/MedEd/medicine/Allergy/Asthma/asthws15.html> (June 27, 2005); "Asthma Action Plan," New York State Department of Health, <http://www.health.state.ny.us/nysdoh/asthma/pdf/4850.pdf> (June 28, 2005).

Chapter 7. Asthma and the Future

1. Andy Fell, "Primate Research Shows Link Between Ozone Pollution, Asthma," *Dateline UC Davis*, October 13, 2000, <http://www.dateline.ucdavis.edu/101300/DL_asthma.html> (March 28, 2005).

2. Environmental Defense, "Pollution Solutions," © 2005, <http://www.environmentaldefense.org/cleanairforlife.cfm?subnav=ps_overview> (March 29, 2005).

3. U.S. Environmental Protection Agency, "Clean Air Interstate Rule," March 10, 2005, <http://www.epa.gov/cair/> (March 29, 2005).

4. Environmental Defense, "Pollution Solutions."

5. Environmental Defense, "Pollution Solutions: Traffic," © 2005, <http://www.environmentaldefense.org/cleanairforlife.cfm?subnav=ps_traffic> (March 29, 2005).

6. Environmental Defense, "Dirty Air & Your Health: Asthma and Air Pollution," © 2005, <http://www.environmentaldefense.org/cleanairforlife.cfm?subnav=da_asthma> (March 29, 2005).

7. "Current NIAID Research Highlights: Specialized Genes May Be Key to Chronic Asthma," March 2, 2005, <http://www2.niaid.nih.gov/newsroom/focuson/asthma01/research.htm> (March 11, 2005).

8. The Wellcome Trust, "Asthma Susceptibility Gene Discovered," May 19, 2003, <http://www.wellcome.ac.uk/en/genome/genesandbody/hg06n008.html> (March 26, 2005).

9. Amy Reyes, "Asthma Gene Clusters Identified," February 8, 2005, <http://www.cincinnatichildrens.org/about/news/release/2005/2-asthma-gene.htm> (March 26, 2005).

10. HealthDayNews, "Asthma: Gene Variant Protects," October 22, 2004, <http://www.health24.com/news/Asthma/1-892,29816.asp> (March 26, 2005).

11. BBC News, "Asthma Vaccine Hope," October 27, 2001, <http://news.bbc.co.uk/1/hi/health/1622057.stm> (March 20, 2005).

12. Canadian Press, "Singapore Researchers Develop Gene-Based Asthma Vaccine: Report," July 12, 2004, <http://mediresource.sympatico.ca/channel_health_news_detail.asp?channel_id=139&menu_item_id=0&news_id=4365> (March 29, 2005).

13. Shane McGlaun, "Asthma Vaccine on the Horizon?" January 6, 2005, <http://asthma.about.com/od/justdiagnosedwithasthma/a/asthmavaccine.htm> (March 30, 2005).

Glossary

airways—The tubes through which air flows to the lungs.

allergen—A substance that causes an allergic reaction.

allergy—An overreaction of the immune system to a normally harmless substance.

alveoli (sing. **alveolus**)—The tiny air sacs in the lungs where gas exchange takes place.

antibodies—Special proteins produced by white blood cells; some antibodies help to kill germs.

asthma—Also called **bronchial asthma**; a disease in which the air passages in the lungs become inflamed, making breathing difficult.

bronchi (sing. **bronchus**)—The larger air tubes leading into the lungs.

bronchioles—Smaller air tubes in the lungs that branch off from the bronchi.

bronchodilator—A drug that opens (dilates) the airways during an asthma attack.

bronchospasm—A sudden narrowing of the muscles in the airway walls.

chronic—Lasting for years or possibly a lifetime.

cilia—Tiny hairlike structures in the lining of the airways that move back and forth, sweeping foreign particles up and out to the throat.

dander—Flakes of dead skin from animals; may be an allergic trigger.

decongestant—A drug that reduces swelling in the breathing passages.

dust mites—Microscopic bugs that feed on the flakes of dead skin in house dust; people may be allergic to dust mite droppings.

exhale—To breathe air out of the lungs.

genes—Chemicals inside each cell that carry inherited traits.

histamine—A chemical released in the body that causes tissues to become inflamed in an allergic reaction.

hyperreactive—"Twitchy"; tending to react (produce symptoms) to a substance that does not bother people with healthy lungs.

IgE—The kind of antibody involved in fighting allergens.

IgG—The kind of antibody involved in fighting germs.

immune system—The body's disease-fighting system, including white blood cells.

immunotherapy—Treatment with a substance that improves the work of the immune system.

inflammation—Redness and swelling as a result of damage or an allergic reaction.

inhale—To breathe air into the lungs.

inhaler—A device that creates a mist of a drug that can be drawn directly into the lungs.

inherited—Passed on by genes from parents to children.

lungs—Two balloonlike organs used for breathing.

mast cell—A special cell in the skin and the lining tissues (such as the tissues in the breathing passages). Mast cells bind to IgEs and release histamine and other inflammation chemicals.

mold—A fungus that grows on rotting plant or animal matter; may be an allergic trigger.

nebulizer—A device that turns liquid into a mist; a type of inhaler.

peak flow meter—A handheld device that measures how fast air flows out of the lungs when a person exhales quickly.

pharynx—Throat.

RAST—*Radioallergosorbent test*, a blood test for specific kinds of IgEs to show sensitivity to particular allergens.

respiratory system—The organs involved in breathing, from the nose to the lungs.

sensitization—Development of an allergy after repeated exposure to an allergen.

spirometer—A machine that measures how much and how fast air goes in and out of a person's airways; used to perform the breathing test, spirometry.

steroid—A type of anti-inflammatory drug.

stethoscope—An instrument used to detect sounds in the chest or other parts of the body.

trachea—The windpipe; the breathing tube that connects the nose and mouth to the bronchi.

trigger—A substance or condition (such as dust or a cold) that brings on an asthma attack.

wheeze—A whistling sound heard when a person breathes through narrowed airways.

Further Reading

Allen, Julian Lewis, Tyra Bryant-Stephens, Nicholas A. Pawlowski, with Sheila Buff and Martha M. Jablow, eds. *The Children's Hospital of Philadelphia Guide to Asthma.* Hoboken, N.J.: John Wiley & Sons, Inc., 2004.

Berger, William. *Asthma for DUMMIES.* Hoboken, N.J.: Wiley Publishing, Inc., 2004.

Gold, Milton, ed. *The Complete Kid's Allergy and Asthma Guide.* Toronto, Canada: Robert Rose, Inc., 2003.

Internet Addresses

(See also **For More Information**, p. 111)

Galatas, John D., MD. "Famous Asthmatics,"
October 14, 2005.
<http://members.tripod.com/~limnos/index-2.
html>.

HealthCentersOnline. "AllergyHealthOnline."
<http://allergy.healthcentersonline.com>.
Articles about allergies and asthma, plus news,
quizzes, animations, and patient stories.

Index

cat allergy, 56–57
chest X-ray, 64
Children's Asthma Research
    Institute and Hospital
    (CARIH), 24
children with asthma, 14
Chinese remedies, 18
chronic asthma, 100
cigarette smoke, 26, 64, 84
cilia, 37, 41, 84
Cincinnati Children's Hospital
    Medical Center, 101
Clean Air Act of 1990, 96
Clean Air Interstate Rule
    (CAIR), 96
cockroach droppings, 6, 44
cockroaches, 82
cold air, 26, 48
colds and flu, 81–83
cold weather, 14
controller medications, 73
control of asthma, 14
Cookson, William, 100
Coolio, **13**
cough, **36**, 37
coughing, 6, 10, 37, 40, 62, 92

D
dander, 6, 26, 43–44, 56, 79, 81
diarrhea, 44
Dickens, Charles, 13
diesel engines, 96, 98
Djukanovic, Ratko, 102
DNA, 51, 100, 103
dust, 12, 26, 37, 39, 42–43, 55
dust mites, 6, 42, 66, 79, 80, 82
dust-proof covers, 80

E
early warning signs, 90–92
Ebers Papyrus, 18
eggs, 44, 79
emotion, 46–47
Environmental Defense, 96
Environmental Protection
    Agency (EPA), 46, 96
ephedrine, 18
exercise, 14, 26, 47–48, 60,
    86–87, 105
exercise-induced asthma, 75
exercise-induced bronchospasm
    (EIB), 48, 86, 87, 89

F
factory smokestacks, 96
Floyer, Sir John, 21
food allergies, 44, 84
food diary, 84

G
Galen, 19–21
genes, 51, 52–53, 100–101
Glass, Susanna, 50
Glass, William, 50

H
hay fever, 43, 55
HEPA filter (high-efficiency
    particulate air filter), 80, 86
heredity, 21, 49, 52–53, 106
Hippocrates, 19
histamine, 26, 56, **57**, 74, 75
hives, 44
Hogshead, Nancy, 13, **58**, 59–62
Hope, Bob, 13
Hurst, Allan, 24
Hyde, Dallas, 94, **95**

I

immune response, 32
immune system, 32, 47, 54–55, 88
immunity to disease, 55
immunoglobulin E (IgE), 24, 55–56, 66, 75, 83
immunoglobulin G (IgG), 54
immunotherapy, 87–89
infections, 46
inflammation, 26, 32, 39–40, 56, 73, 75, 101
inhaler, 6, 10–11, 22–23, 29, 69, **70**, 74
irritants, 44–45, 84–85
Ishizaka, Kimishige, 24, **25**
Ishizaka, Teruko, 24, **25**
Itkin, Irving, 26

J

Joel, Billy, 13
Joyner-Kersee, Jackie, 13, 30, **31**
Judd, Wynonna, **8**, 9–12

K

Kennedy, John F., 13
Kennedy, Patrick, 13

L

Lavigne, Avril, **13**
long-acting bronchodilators, 74
long-term control medicines, 73–74
Louganis, Greg, 13
lungs, 33, **34**, 35, 48, 84, 105

M

ma huang, 18
Maimonides, 21
mast cells, 56, **57**, 75
medical history, 63
Mexico City, 45, 94, **97**
mild intermittent asthma, 67
mild persistent asthma, 68
Minnelli, Liza, 13
moderate persistent asthma, 68
mold, 6, 12, 26, 42, **43**, 55, 81
Mt. Etna, **20**
mucus, 19–21, 36–37, 39–40, 48, 84

N

nasal decongestants, 74
National Home for Jewish Children, 23
National Institutes of Health, 26
nebulizer, 30, 69, 71, **72**, 74
nighttime symptoms, 62, 67, 68
nitrogen dioxide, 46

O

Olympics, 59, 99
outgrowing asthma, 63, 105
oxygen, 33–36, 48, 84, 94
ozone, 46, 93, 94
ozone levels, 93–96, 99

P

particulates, 46
Paul of Aegina, 21
peak flow, 89, 106
peak flow meter, 60, **65**, 89–**91**
peanuts, 44, 79
Peshkin, M. Murray, 23
pets, 81, 82–83
pharynx, **34**, 35
Platts-Mills, Thomas, **82**
pneumococcal pneumonia, 83

pollen, 6, 12, 36, 42, 43, 55, **57**, 79, 80
pollen counts, 80
preventing asthma attacks, 7, 74, 77–92

Q

quick-relief medicine, 71. *See also* rescue medication.

R

ragweed, 43
RAST (Radioallergosorbent test), 66
rescue medication, 71, 78
respiratory system, **34**, 35
rhesus monkeys, 93, 103
rodent urine, 44
Rodman, Dennis, 13
Roosevelt, Theodore, 13, 15–**17**, 18

S

Salter, Henry Hyde, 22
Scorsese, Martin, 13
secondhand smoke, 85
sensitization, 57
severe persistent asthma, 68
severity of asthma, 67–68
shortness of breath, 6, 39, 62
skin testing, 66
Smith, Emmitt, 13
smog, 45
smog-alert days, 94
smoke, 39
sneeze, **36**, 37
spirometer, 64, 65
spirometry, 64
spores, 43

sports, 105
steroids, 73, 74
St. Louis Children's Hospital, 77, 78
Stone, Sharon, 13
stress, 26, 46
Strunk, Robert, **78**
sulfur dioxide, 46

T

Taylor, Elizabeth, 13
theophylline, 22
tightness in the chest, 6, 40, 92
tobacco smoke, 22, 44
trachea, **34**, 35
traffic pollution, 98
treatment plan, 67, 76, 106
Tristan da Cunha, 49–51
twin studies, 53
twitchy lungs, 26, 32, 53, 106

U

University of California, Davis (UC Davis), 93

V

Van Dyken, Amy, 30
vomiting, 44

W

weather, 46
wheat, 44
wheezing, 6, 12, 37, 39–40, 62, 106
white blood cells, 54

X

Xolair (omalizumab), 75–76